INSIDER STRATEGIES TO BECOMING A GREAT FLIRT.
DO YOU KNOW...?

- ♥ How to deliver a sexy handshake.
- ♥ Four flirting secrets that will really get you noticed.
- ♥ The one simple object every successful flirt needs to carry.
- ♥ Flirtatious maneuvers that can change your outlook, your attitude, and even your life.

In this wise and witty guide, a master flirt teaches all the skills you need to enhance self-confidence, sharpen communication, and help you approach new people with assurance. It won't be long before you fill up your social calendar with interesting friends, professional contacts, dates—or a lifelong partner.

SUSAN G. RABIN, M.A., is a relationship therapist, communication and flirting coach, international speaker, and president of Dynamic Communications, Inc., a company dedicated to making relationships work and is director of The School of Flirting®. She appears frequently on radio and television, including *The Oprah Winfrey Show, The Today Show, Good Morning America, The O'Reilly Report,* as well as on the Learning Channel and CNN. Susan was the former Family Living/Sex Education Coordinator for the New York City Board of Education, and is the author of *How to Attract Anyone, Anytime, Anyplace* and *Lucky in Love* (both available in Plume editions). She lives and works in New York City.

Visit www.dynamiccommunications.com and www.schoolofflirting.com

BARBARA LAGOWSKI is a former editor and the author of fourteen books.

Also by Susan Rabin with Barbara Lagowski
How to Attract Anyone, Anytime, Anyplace
Cyberflirt

1·0·1
Ways to Flirt

How to Get More Dates
and Meet Your Mate

♥

SUSAN RABIN

with
Barbara Lagowski

Ⓟ

A PLUME BOOK

PLUME

Published by the Penguin Group
Penguin Books USA Inc., 375 Hudson Street, New York, New York 10014, U.S.A.
Penguin Books Ltd, 27 Wrights Lane, London W8 5TZ, England
Penguin Books Australia Ltd, Ringwood, Victoria, Australia
Penguin Books Canada Ltd, 10 Alcorn Avenue, Toronto, Ontario, Canada M4V 3B2
Penguin Books (N.Z.) Ltd, 182–190 Wairau Road, Auckland 10, New Zealand

Penguin Books Ltd, Registered Offices:
Harmondsworth, Middlesex, England

First Published by Plume, an imprint of Dutton Signet, a division of Penguin Books USA Inc.

First Printing, January, 1997
15 16 17 18 19 20

Copyright © Susan Rabin, 1997
All rights reserved

Library of Congress Cataloging-in-Publication Data
Rabin, Susan.
101 ways to flirt : how to get more dates and meet your mate /
Susan Rabin with Barbara Lagowski.
p. cm.
ISBN 0-452-27685-3
1. Interpersonal relations. 2. Interpersonal attraction. 3. Man-woman relationships.
I. Lagowski, Barbara J. II. Title.
HM132.R23 1997
646.7'7—dc20 96-43265 CIP

Printed in the United States of America
Set in Garamond
Designed by Jesse Cohen

To all my readers who made my first book a bestseller and requested yet another. Thanks for your appreciation and inspiration. May you enjoy and learn from *101 Ways to Flirt* as you did from *How to Attract Anyone, Anytime, Anyplace.*

To all my new readers, I hope you enjoy this book as your introduction to the "art of flirting" and will want to refer to *How to Attract Anyone, Anytime, Anyplace* for more helpful hints to becoming The Master Flirt.

To Penguin books for establishing my credibility and success in the field of interpersonal relationships. To family, friends, Stuart, Kristin, Jeff and Frannie for being proud and enjoying my success.

Acknowledgments

I wish to acknowledge the myriad of readers who let me know how much they enjoyed *How to Attract Anyone, Anytime, Anyplace*, and how that book empowered them to reach out, have more fun, and change their lives. I hope this book, "101 Ways to Flirt," continues the process of "becoming."

Thanks, Sandra Martin. You are the best agent and friend a flirt can have.

Thanks to Peter Borland, my editor of *How to Attract Anyone, Anytime, Anyplace*. He engaged me with his ideas for *101 Ways to Flirt*.

Thank you to Jennifer Moore, my current editor, who has shown her enthusiasm and belief in this project.

Thanks, Barbara Lagowski. We are of one voice. It is a pleasure working with you again. Let's keep doing it, Barbara.

Thanks to my friends and family. Our relationships fuel my fire.

Thanks to all the men and women who have touched my life and allowed me to flirt with them daily. Life is so much fun when you relate positively to people, and even unpleasant communications can be turned around with skilled flirting.

Flirting: 101 Ways to Just Do It!

One morning, while boarding a train to Philadelphia, I was confronted with a decision. In the aisle seat immediately to my left, there was a nice-looking man rummaging through his briefcase. Sitting with him might give me an opportunity to flirt. In the rear of the car there were more empty seats than I could count. Choosing one of them would give me a desperately needed hour and a half of peace and quiet. What would I do . . . take a risk? Or take a nap? The other passengers were kneecapping me now with their luggage in an effort to pass through the narrow aisle. Throwing caution to the wind, I slid into the window seat facing the handsome man.

Minutes later, the train chugged out of the station—and I was already certain I had made the wrong choice. Although my seatmate did not speak to me directly, his body language was making me feel very unwelcome. He would neither catch my gaze nor return my smile. He fidgeted constantly in his seat as if something (or somebody!) was making him terribly uncomfortable. Embarrassed that I might be the cause of this much misery, I hid behind my morning paper, peeking at my fellow traveler from behind the op-ed page. When I saw him pull a popular biography out of his bag, I hoped that he might finally relax. Instead, he squinted his eyes at the page, as though he were trying to read in a dark cave.

I simply couldn't stand his discomfort any longer. I laid my paper in my lap, smiled at him, and asked, as pleasantly as possible, "You seem to be having trouble reading. Would you like me to move so you can sit closer to the window?"

At first, he seemed startled. Then his demeanor softened. "Thanks for asking, but it's really not the light. The fact is, I don't like train travel very much. I don't like train seats, train noise, or even the way trains move. Unfortunately, my job requires a lot of train travel. So you see my dilemma."

I said I understood. Then I asked what he was (or wasn't) currently reading—and the conversation was off and running. He told me that he always read historical biographies —except when he was reading and rereading the manuscript he was working on. I told him that I had recently published my first book, *How to Attract Anyone, Anytime, Anyplace*, and that the experience had been worth every bit of the anxiety and hard work that had gone into it. Before we knew it, we had discussed everything from agents to word-processing programs and the train was pulling into Philadelphia. We exchanged business cards at the car door.

So, did my personal version of "Strangers on a Train" turn out to be a nonstop to romance—or a derailment? Neither, really. Although my new friend called two days later just to let me know that the rest of his trip paled in comparison to the portion of it he shared with me, and although we met for a very pleasant lunch in his hometown of Washington, D.C., the miles between us made it impossible to connect romantically. Still, the story of my Metroliner encounter has helped me to connect with countless singles anxious to get on the fast track to successful flirting—not because it is a perfect love story, but because it illustrates perfectly the three most important truths every flirt needs to know to get to "hello" and beyond, approach new prospects with confidence, and attract anyone, anytime, anyplace. They are:

Flirting is a conscious choice. It is not "something that just happens when the chemistry is right." If I had spent two hours on that train doing crossword puzzles, I might have added a few new words to my vocabulary, but I would never have added the name of a new and charming prospect to my little black book. And until you allow yourself the freedom to flirt, you probably won't either.

There's no right time or place to flirt. A bus stop, the local dog run, the tax accountant's office, or inside a noisy train car may not seem like the most romantic places in the world. But anyplace you meet that special someone becomes a special place to you. Be prepared to flirt with whomever you meet wherever you are and you're guaranteed to meet interesting men and women everywhere you go. Limit yourself to singles' events or particular bars and you limit your playing field—and your potential as a flirt.

Last but not least, *flirting is the art of interacting with others without serious intent.* The only bells and whistles I heard on the Metroliner that day were safety signals . . . but I can't say I was disappointed. Although I didn't meet "that certain someone" on that particular outing, I did add an interesting new contact to my social network and that's always a sign of a good day's flirting. I've heard from many flirts who have used the skills they learned in my first book to find fascinating friends, casual companions, professional contacts . . . and yes, lifelong partners. And my strategies will do the same for you if you think of flirting as a playful, unpredictable adventure rather than a ticket to commitment.

The more than five thousand flirts who have attended my seminars and workshops—many of whom have contributed stories you will read in this book—have learned that flirting is not a natural talent that some people have and others do not. It is an easily acquired skill that enhances self-confidence, sharpens communication, enables them to approach new contacts with assurance, and fills their lives (and their social calendars!) with a constant supply of interesting, creative new contacts.

I know that wherever you are, with whomever you choose to meet, the tips, techniques, and stories in this book will work for you. Just choose to flirt, decide to make any-place work for you, and you'll be off, running, and devising your own ingenious, irresistible ways to flirt!

♥ **1** ♥

3 Irrational Fears That Keep Potentially Great Flirts from Flirting

1. *"I'm afraid that making the first move will make me seem desperate or sexually aggressive."*

   Not if you don't confuse flirting with seduction or teasing. Seduction and sexual teasing are manipulative and, yes, even desperate in nature. What motivates this sort of encounter is the seducer's need to coerce someone else into fulfilling his needs. Flirting, on the other hand, is a charming and honest expression of interest in another person. Its goal is to bring out the best in someone else so you can appreciate each other for as long as the encounter lasts. The subtle skills you will learn in this book will make you seem accessible, confident, and on top of your form—not needy, predatory, and on the make.

2. *"I'm afraid that others won't find me attractive."*

My thirty-nine-year-old friend Mitch is an aesthetically challenged flirt. He has shaggy shoulder-length hair, a chipped front tooth, and a nose only a plastic surgeon could love. He also has a seemingly endless supply of female admirers. Why? Because no one is more interesting and attractive than someone who can make *others* feel interesting and attractive. That's not to say that you will never encounter a shortsighted someone who rejects you because you don't have Pamela Anderson's hair—or any hair at all. You may. But that will be his or her loss. With the skills you will learn in this book, you can simply move on to a more appreciative prospect.

3. *"I'm afraid I'll say something stupid."*

How stupid is "Can you believe it? Here I was trying not to splash Gatorade on you and I ended up splashing mud on you!" Not your idea of a suave opening line? It worked for a friend of mine who was holding an open drink container while riding a bike (don't drink and drive!) and swerved into a puddle to avoid drenching a woman who meandered into his path. He paid for her dry-cleaning and she reciprocated with lunch.

Some of the most dynamic and longest-lasting relationships I know began with an off-beat, unexpected, or downright silly comment. So is it stupid to ask "Do you think it will rain?" while you're trekking through Death Valley in August? Not if it begins a conversation.

3 More Irrational Fears That Keep Potentially Great Flirts from Flirting

1. *"I can't deal with rejection."*

Yes, you can. In fact, you've been successfully dealing with rejection all of your life! Remember that neighborhood ball game when you weren't chosen to play on anybody's side? Sure, you were hurt, but you picked up your glove and went looking for a more amicable group of kids to play with. And remember that to-die-for man you zeroed in on in a nightclub? It took you all night to work up enough courage to ask him to dance—and he shot you down like an enemy bomber. Who knows whatever happened to him (something awful if there's anything to the idea of karma) but you're still dancing, aren't you?

Everyone in the world—from rocket scientists to rock collectors, from Queen Latifah to Princess Diana—has experienced rejection. What we have all learned from these experiences is that rejection is disappointing, painful, and sometimes embarrassing, but it is never fatal, final, or a reason not to flirt.

2. *"I'm afraid the person I flirt with will not be my type."*

   And I'm afraid that by editing out so many eligible singles without the benefit of even a "how do you do" you're cheating yourself out of the pure pleasure of flirting! Flirting is not a serious, goal-oriented task. And it is not the fast track to a lifelong commitment. If you are saving your flirting skills for a fantasy man or woman who exists, to date, only in your dreams, you might think you're saving yourself a little time. What you're really doing is denying yourself the possibility of a stimulating conversation, a brief respite from a dull party, or just a little ego boost.

   By the way, the possibility also exists that someone who doesn't look like your type might actually *be* your type. But if you exclude prospects on the basis of their appearance, their accoutrements, or their manner, you will never find out.

3. *"I just got out of a relationship that lasted too long. I don't want any entanglements."*

   Then flirting is the pastime for you! The art of acting

and interacting *without serious intent*, flirting will enable you to meet the intriguing people who share your interests without requiring that you share their bed, their debts, or their life. On the personal level, flirting will shake you out of the post-breakup doldrums, enable you to communicate your feelings (including your temporary desire to avoid intense relationships), and make you a skilled interpreter of others' messages. (If she wants a long-term commitment, you'll know!) In the professional sphere, flirting skills will help you advance your career, gain the attention and cooperation of others, and turn balky clients into supportive colleagues.

♥ 3 ♥

How to Make Yourself Approachable

Lesson One: Divide and Conquer

*W*edding bells will never break up that old gang of yours as long as you continue to travel in a pack! Women: You may be a one-in-a-million find, but few men are willing to wend their way past even a few of your closest friends to find you! And men—before you join that he-man huddle in the corner of the room, remember: No woman is likely to rush a defensive line of your best buddies.

There may be safety in numbers, but safety is a poor substitute for an active social life. The next time you're invited to a party or an event, take the risk and go it alone. You may discover that flying solo is not as daunting as you've imagined. Or, if you really can't face the thought of socializing by yourself, arrange with your friends to separate for an hour or so. That will give any admirers an opportunity to approach without having to "play to an audience," or infiltrate your entourage.

♥ 4 ♥
How to Make Yourself Approachable

Lesson Two: To Meet Interesting People,
Be an Interesting Person

"*B*e an interesting person?" Tony, a man I met after one of my seminars, asked. "It's not possible. Interesting people are born, not made." In fact, as I explained to Tony, interesting people are neither born *nor* made. They are continually engaged in the process of *becoming*.

So, how can you be all that you can be without enlisting in the Army? Take a class, learn to windsurf, volunteer for a charity, become a vegetarian, go to a local psychic fair or the next *Star Trek* convention, join Parents Without Partners or another single's group, attend a seminar, go to a poetry reading, or take those dance lessons you're sorry you opted out of as a teenager! These and countless other activities you can tap into right now will not only make you a more intriguing, well-rounded person, they will put you into proximity with hundreds of people who share your interests, give you plenty of fodder for spontaneous conversation, and make you a blissfully approachable flirt!

So try your hand at throwing pottery (hint: Throw it while the clay's still wet), enroll in a photography class, host a wine tasting, do anything you like . . . just get out of the house and do it! Pursuing a hobby that stimulates you will give you insight into your own fascinating personality—and it might even put you within striking range of that very special person who would make your life complete.

♥ 5 ♥
How to Make Yourself Approachable

Lesson Three: Smile, Darn Ya, Smile!

*I*f you read my first book, *How to Attract Anyone, Anytime, Anyplace*, you'll no doubt remember my friend Leslie, a natural-born flirt and executive assistant who gave such "good phone" she got dates on the basis of her voice alone. Well, I am proud to say that Leslie has since outdone herself. On a recent afternoon, in less than one hour, she met three charming men at the Museum of Modern Art! How did a forty-something flirt accomplish such a feat in a city full of gorgeous, available women? "I smile a lot," she explained. "You see, I'm something of a people collector. I like to hear other people's life stories. And I like to find out what makes them tick. So, wherever I am, I make it a point to smile at the men and women who pass by. If they're in the mood for a chat, they stop. If not . . .

well, let's just say the best thing about being a people collector is that there's no shortage of people."

If 90 percent of the available men in Manhattan took the A train into oblivion tomorrow, there would still be no shortage of people for easy, approachable flirts like Leslie to collect. And there won't be for you, either, once you stop saving your smiles for people you know and start sharing them with the people you *want* to know.

This single flirting tip can change your attitude, your outlook (research shows that smiling makes us feel better!), and your life. Promise yourself that you'll smile at at least five strangers each day and soon you'll have a people collection of your own.

♥ **6** ♥

The One Line to Have
When You're Having More Than One

I was waiting for a friend in a crowded hotel bar when a debonair gentleman caught my eye. And I'm glad he did. Without noticing me, or speaking a single word to me, he taught me a very memorable lesson in flirting.

The man did not rush the bar like most people do when they enter a busy establishment, but lingered briefly near the doorway and scanned the crowd. Clearly, he was looking for an opportunity to flirt. But how? The only woman in the place that seemed to interest him was otherwise engaged . . . in conversation with a female friend. What was he going to do?

The question turned out to be more of a brainteaser for me than it was for this old pro. He walked confidently up to the ladies' table, smiled his most winning smile, and said simply, "May I buy you two lovely ladies a drink?"

It was a stroke of genius! The man knew from experience that waiting for two chums to separate could be futile. So he made his move. And, of course, the women accepted. The man's genteel, inclusive approach threatened neither their friendship, their ethics, nor their plans.

Since that evening, I've shared this nonthreatening, thirst-quenching, and liberating (Women: Do use it on two gentlemen!) line with all of my seminars. Of course, I still prefer to do my relating on a one-to-one basis. But if you can't beat the herd, join the herd!

♥ 7 ♥

Arresting Glances That Won't Get You Arrested

*E*ach time our eyes meet someone else's, even for a split second, we send a message. Since eye contact is the first contact we make with the available men and women around us, it is critical that the messages we send are always positive and affirming rather than confrontational or threatening. How can we use our eyes to make the people we meet reach for their date books rather than a can of mace?

- ♥ To make your motives understood, eye contact should always be accompanied by an amiable—not lecherous or leering—smile.
- ♥ Check your body language. If you're leaning toward your new acquaintance or encroaching on his or her personal space, you may be perceived as too aggressive.

♥ Communicate nothing other than friendliness. That means no winking, no "woo-woo" eyebrow raises, and absolutely no peeking at body parts between the neck and knees.

♥ Beware of very brief, darting glances. They can make even the most sincere flirt appear shifty and suspicious.

♥ Don't allow a lingering look to linger too long. In the animal kingdom, staring is a ploy large carnivores use to mesmerize their prey before an attack. And good flirts never attack!

♥ 8 ♥
Quick Fix: The Flirting Triangle

"*He wasn't drop-dead gorgeous. He wasn't dressed like he just stepped off the cover of GQ. Nevertheless, a man on the elevator caught my eye . . . until I caught his. Then he started staring down at a glob of mud on the elevator floor as if it were the Rosetta Stone. What did I do wrong?*"

Lesson: Many flirts believe that the eyes are, indeed, the windows to the soul. You can imagine, then, how unnerved those flirts must feel to discover that someone is staring into their windows!

To take the hard focus off eye contact, I suggest that you use the Flirting Triangle Technique to broaden your target area. Think of your partner's face as a triangle with the widest points at the corners of his forehead and tapering down to the tip of his chin. Now, instead of staring directly into your partner's eyes, allow your glance to wander from his brow to his temples; from his earlobe to his chin. Now and then, allow your gazes to meet—you might even acknowledge him with a slight smile or nod—then continue with your exploration, moving your eyes over his face lightly, playfully, and always respectfully.

At first this technique may seem strange to you. If you are the direct, "eye-to-eye" type, it may not even seem like real eye contact to you. But researchers have discovered that these brief, literally "glancing" eye movements are actually the first steps in the complex dance that leads to intimacy. Isn't it worth learning a few new moves?

Lingering Looks:
How Long Is Long Enough?

*D*irect eye-to-eye contact should communicate this simple statement: "Hello. I see you." Catch your partner's eye for about as long as it would take for you to say that phrase aloud and he or she will be eager to meet your gaze again. Hold it a millisecond longer and he or she will be eager . . . to get out of your range.

♥ **10** ♥

Why Good Flirts Don't Ever Make Eye Contact with Body Parts Other Than the Eyes

♥ Because getting "checked out" diminishes a woman's personhood.

♥ Because men are more than the estimated sum of their parts.

♥ Because bodies are not always what they are propped up to be.

♥ Because when sexual scrutiny begins, friendly flirtation ends.

♥ Because although great buns may "call to you," they cannot actually converse with you.

♥ Because you *will* get caught.

♥ **11** ♥

Looking for Love at the Local Launderette

♥ Wash your clothes at night. It's a singles crowd.

♥ There is nothing more boring than sitting in a laundromat waiting for a load of towels to spin. Set yourself apart from the drips by bringing along something you and your fellow clean freaks can do to pass the time. One flirt I know increased his popularity tenfold by bringing in a stack of browsable magazines and inviting everyone to help themselves. Another had good luck with a handheld video game that could be set for more than one player. Still another, an elementary school teacher, actually got several people to spend an hour on the laundromat *floor* tracing and cutting out paper shapes for a second-grade holiday project.

♥ When in doubt about the procedure or the equipment, don't ask the manager—ask the hottest prospect in the place. If you know everything there is about doing laundry, including the comparative merits of Biz and Duz, make sure you don't have the right change.

♥ Don't be a tightwad. If that attractive stranger's drier shuts off before the clothes are dry, be generous and toss in a couple of coins. When he or she comes back, confess your random act of kindness but accept nothing in return.

Note to men: Don't think you're doing a woman a favor by removing her dry clothes from the machine and folding them for her. No woman is happy to learn that a strange man has been rummaging through her skivvies.

♥ 12 ♥
Outrageous Flirting Tactics
That Really Worked!

The Switcheroo

"*One night I went to a club with a few friends. We had barely chosen a table when I noticed a man standing near the bar who was staring at me. An hour later, he was still staring at me—and I had come down with an acute case of the creeps. Halfway through the evening, the DJ cued up a slow dance and the absolute worst happened: The man walked over to my table and asked me to dance. Without thinking (I'm usually a pretty shy person!) I turned toward the handsome man who was seated at the next table, grabbed his hand, and explained to my stalker, 'I'd love to dance with you but I've already been asked.' Then I pulled my rescuer onto the dance floor where I explained my fears and my behavior. We ended up dancing all night and making a date for the following day!*"

Lesson: People *love* helping others. Why? Because coming to someone's aid—even if it's only to give directions—makes one feel competent, needed, and fully human. While a bold move like this one might have been out of character for you, it lets your new friend know that you perceived him to be approachable, attractive, and trustworthy. Moreover, the drama of the moment acted as a natural icebreaker for you, giving you both plenty to chat about once the music ended. Good move!

The Signals She Sends When She Wants to Know You Better

A friend recently told me about a particularly embarrassing first date she had endured at a drive-through safari park. My friend and her date didn't know each other well. Nor did they know each other any better at the end of their safari. But they came away from the experience knowing a great deal about the mating rituals of ostriches in captivity—and how captive two human beings can feel when surrounded by large birds in the throes of passion.

The mating dance performed by men and women is intricate, fascinating, and usually more socially acceptable. It is also made up of movements so easily recognizable that even a fledgling flirt can interpret them.

These include:

The Smile. If you've been flirting any length of time, you know that smiles can be merely polite, professional, and practiced, or overtly insincere. How can you tell those pasted-on grins from the smile that says "I like you"? By the temperature. The sincere smile is always warm and makes you feel at ease.

Short, Repetitive Glances. It means "Of all the faces in this crowd, yours is the most interesting to me." When she glances in your direction again, be sure to smile.

The Fixed Glance. If she holds your gaze while conversing with you, she has decided that she likes what she's hearing —and what she's seeing.

The Hair Flip, The Head Toss, and *The Lip Lick*. She finds you attractive and hopes you are as intrigued with her.

The Whisper and *The Lean*. If she leans toward you in conversation or whispers, thereby causing you to lean toward her, she is inviting you to share her personal space. By all means, move closer but don't make any overt physical moves. Touch is a touchy subject for most women and it only takes one false move to turn that intimate whisper into a stony silence.

♥ **14** ♥

The Signals He Sends When
He Wants to Know You Better

Unfortunately for female flirts, researchers simply don't know as much about men's nonverbal signals as they do about women's. That's because flirting among homo sapiens has only recently become recognized as a true, biologically based science and there is still a great deal of research to be done. It may also have a great deal to do with the belief among social scientists that women—not men—are the initiators of nonverbal flirtation and therefore the primary generators of attraction signals. (In other words, he may make the phone call but she has already sent the message!)

Nevertheless, men do make their intentions known. Often they signal their interest in the same ways as women do. (The Smile and the Lean are equal-opportunity techniques!)

But they have also developed their own unique nonverbal repertoire, including a host of gentlemanly gestures such as:

The Tie Stroke. The tie stroke (or the lapel smooth) is the male equivalent of a woman's lip lick. Anthropologists call this sort of signaling "preening behavior." The message it sends is "I like you and I want to make the best impression possible."

The Eyebrow Flash. The eyes may be the windows of the soul but if you want to know what a man is really thinking, check those brows. If they're relaxed, even limp, you're not his cup of tea. But if he is wide-eyed with brows flashing upward, it's a sure sign that you've taken him by surprise—and he couldn't be more delighted!

The Arm Guide. You may perceive the arm guide as an expression of good manners. Achieved with barely a touch (and sometimes no physical contact at all!), this gesture can pass as nothing more than a polite way of directing a new acquaintance through an uncomfortably crowded room—but don't be fooled. A man who uses the arm guide is a man who doesn't want to lose you among the other party guests. He is also a man who wants any other interested males to know that you are being "taken care of" and are therefore off-limits.

♥ **15** ♥

How to Make Flirting the Main Attraction at the Amusement Park

♥ Never go to an amusement park in even-numbered groups. It cheats you out of the opportunity to yell, "Single? Right here!" when the attendant is looking to fill a ride that's strictly two to a car. With a little planning (and a strong stomach!), finding your significant other can literally be a roller-coaster ride.

♥ If you are a single parent or a single who doesn't consider kids a barrier to romance, don't pass up those stunt shows that are so popular with the under-ten crowd. I've met very lovely men at Disney World, Sea World, and Six Flags simply by engaging their children in conversation. Remember: There are many routes to love, but the way to a single parent's heart is through his or her children.

♥ Win something cuddly and then give it to a lucky bystander. It lets him or her know that you're really the prize.

♥ **16** ♥
How to Warm Up a Snow Day

- ♥ Don't just shovel on the compliments; shovel his or her walk! A little invigorating activity is a great cure for conversational "cold feet." And who knows . . . you may even get invited in for a cup of cocoa.
- ♥ Carry a container of lock defroster. It's a guaranteed icebreaker when that certain someone finds herself unable to budge that frozen car door. (To be a really well-stocked flirt, toss some jumper cables and a bag of deicing crystals in your trunk. Get someone unstuck and they may become stuck on you.)
- ♥ One of the most charming stories about wintertime flirtation came to me from a young woman who lives in Vermont. She was in her kitchen when she noticed a man she'd met briefly at a party walking around in her front

yard. When she rushed to her upstairs bedroom window to get a better view, she noticed that her acquaintance had actually trampled out a message in the snow: "Have toboggan. Please play." She did. And their friendship has been warming up ever since.

♥ 17 ♥
The Five Worst Places to Flirt

♥ During church or religious services. (Some things are still sacred, you know!)

♥ Anywhere that's too dark to use the flirting triangle technique and too secluded for anyone but a felon to see your flirting prop.

♥ The zoo. Animals do the darndest things.

♥ A unisex hair salon. No woman really wants to be noticed when her hair is wet, slathered with chemicals, or wrapped in tinfoil like last night's Moo Goo Gai Pan.

♥ In court. Especially if the case in question is your own divorce.

♥ 18 ♥
Flirting at the Nude Resort

- ♥ Wear a snappy tie or grandmother's pearls to dinner. The right accessories will always set you apart from the underdressed.
- ♥ Forget the reflective sunglasses routine. They're onto it.
- ♥ Invite a group of new acquaintances over for a rollicking game of "Get-Dressed Poker."
- ♥ One word: sunblock.

♥ *19* ♥

Flirting Props: Why You Should Carry One If You Want to Carry On a Conversation

"*L*et's Give Them Something to Talk About" was the hit song on everyone's lips several years ago. But it will always be a favorite of mine because it might have been written about flirting props: those interesting conversation pieces we carry when we want others to talk to us!

A boon for the bashful, a foolproof flirting technique for the terminally tongue-tied, a flirting prop can be virtually anything at all—a jingling charm bracelet, a tie or a T-shirt printed with an Escher design, an umbrella that's big enough for two (great for bus stops!), or even a homemade box kite—as long as it attracts the eye, invites comment, and tells the world how fascinating you are.

Although you'll find dozens of imaginative flirting props

—and suggestions for the most effective places to use them—listed throughout the pages of this book, the flirts in my workshops have told me that the covers of my books are among the best conversation starters of all. Shouldn't you be reading this one where someone special can see you?

♥ 20 ♥
Flirting Props That Attract Anyone, Anytime, Anyplace

♥ Anything out of place. I know a man who enjoyed several conversations with curious women and got a helping hand from two others while carrying a huge wooden toboggan he'd just bought at a yard sale . . . over the Fourth of July weekend.

♥ Tattoos. Tattoos have never been more socially acceptable than they are right now. And because they are considered display art, body embellishments are fair game for unsolicited (but positive!) comment. I would think twice, however, before admiring the body piercings of someone I did not know, particularly if the perforations are located between the neck and the knees.

♥ A sketchbook. Who can resist a peek at a work of art in progress? No one. That's what makes a sketchbook a no-fail flirting prop.

But what about the talent requirement? The reality is that sketching is about line and shape, so all you really need to capture is the general contour of the scenery around you—and the interest of any attractive bystanders. But if you truly don't know a charcoal pencil from a charcoal briquette, try a camera instead. The sound of an instant photo in the making draws curious flirts and you never can tell what will develop while the pictures do. Just make sure you limit your subjects to *scenes* that appeal to you—not people. It's bad form to put your sexual interest in focus.

♥ Memorabilia. Whether you collect Swatch watches, vintage Grateful Dead tie-dyes, or Civil War memorabilia (I know one flirt who goes nowhere without his authentic Confederate soldier's cap), if you've got it, flaunt it! Those in the know will appreciate your collection. And those who aren't will appreciate the opportunity to meet someone who isn't just another face in the crowd.

♥ Media. Can you hit a home run with a radio? You can if you're like my friend Kate, who happened to be the only flirt on the street with a radio during the last game of the 1994 World Series! In a matter of minutes, she met enough men to start her own baseball team.

♥ A unique piece of jewelry. I recently met a woman who

wore only one piece of jewelry: a simple silver bracelet embellished with the words "First Class Bitch." She acknowledged that the piece may have frightened off less intrepid suitors, but it caught the eye of her future husband, who wasn't in the market for a Pollyanna. Another friend, Melissa, invested $1.25 in a child's bubble necklace (a green plastic vial filled with bubble-blowing liquid suspended from a string) and headed for a local single's bar. The bubbles livened the place up. And the necklace gave the quiet, shy men Melissa prefers an opportunity to do what they otherwise could not: express an interest in Melissa by expressing an interest in her flirting prop. My newest flirting prop is a large colored glass ring in different shapes. It makes it easy to start a conversation. Besides having to notice it, it flashes on and off on your command. Singles in my seminar can't resist it. If interested in owning one, write to me.

♥ 21 ♥
Going for It at the Grocery Store

*O*ne of the funniest stories I've ever heard about flirting at the grocery store was passed along to me by a woman who bought my first book, *How to Attract Anyone, Anytime, Anyplace*. She was about halfway through the book when her seventy-year old mother dropped in for a visit. While the woman busied herself in another room, her mother picked the book up from the coffee table and began to scan it. Later that evening, the older woman stopped into a market and, on the spur of the moment, decided to try out some of what she had learned. She checked out the crowd, zeroed in on a good-looking gentleman, and deliberately bumped her shopping cart into his. Of course, my friend's mother apologized profusely, just as I suggested in the book. But when the man stopped, beamed warmly at her, and said, "It's okay. A woman as charming as you can bump your cart into mine anytime!" she became flustered and tongue-tied. She ended up abandoning her cart—and the flirtation—and fleeing from the store. The lesson? My flirting tips really do work—sometimes more effectively than people expect! And you can bag a significant other at the supermarket, too. Just follow these handy shopping tips:

- ♥ Ever wonder who's cruising the aisles of the twenty-four-hour grocery at 9:25 at night? Career-minded singles. Look for them in the produce department (workaholics must keep their energy up!) or chilling among the frozen foods.
- ♥ Buy a live lobster. You'd be surprised how much attention a moving crustacean attracts at the checkout counter.
- ♥ Shop the specialty aisles for a man or woman who shares your interests, nutritional requirements, or even political leanings, then "accidentally" exchange carts with her. "I'm *so* sorry . . . I just saw the brewer's yeast and veggie burgers in the cart and . . . well, naturally I assumed it was mine!"
- ♥ Those do-it-yourself checkout counters with automatic scanners don't just make it easy for clerks—they make it easy for flirts, as well! As simple as they appear, hardly anyone gets through those checkouts without requiring

assistance . . . and canny flirts are always ready to assist! In addition, someone is always leaving their sales slip behind in the automated register. That gives you a good excuse to catch up to the appealing shopper that checked out just before you . . . or to engineer a "chance encounter" with the engaging person in line behind you.

♥ No, it *isn't* politically incorrect to offer help to someone with their heavy packages. It's charming, thoughtful—and an especially pleasant surprise when a woman offers her assistance to an overburdened *man*.

♥ **22** ♥

What Your Grocery-Store Flirting Style Reveals About You

While browsing the produce department of your neighborhood market, you notice an attractive shopper cruising the bins. You immediately:

A. Rush over to the startled shopper, wave a cantaloupe under his/her nose, and announce, "You can't choose a ripe melon by tapping it. You have to smell it. See? This one's ready. I'll put it in your cart for you."

B. Since verbal contact is out of the question (if he wanted a conversation he'd be in a telephone booth, not a grocery store!) you lurk among the Granny Smiths, hoping he'll notice you.

C. Smile and say hello. A bit of interaction makes any mundane task more pleasant.

———————

If the first answer comes closest to your flirting style, you are an Aggressive Flirt. Although your "in your face" methods make it easy for you to *meet* a lot of promising prospects (who could evade you?), your bossiness, superior air, and demanding tone ultimately frighten them away. Remember: Flirting is the fine art of relating to others and allowing others to relate to you. And overpowering is never a substitute for relating.

If answer B best fits your flirting style, you are a Passive Flirt. Can anyone be passive and a flirt at the same time? Not really. Yet that oxymoron is a vivid description of the internal struggle that characterizes the Passive Flirt. He wants desperately to be noticed, but is reluctant to say anything to attract notice. She wants to walk off into the sunset with the man of her dreams—but cannot bring herself to take the first step. Unfortunately, a flirt who does not act is a flirt who does not get. I suggest that you begin to overcome your passivity by smiling at ten strangers a day. Once you've mastered that, promise yourself you'll say hello to ten strangers a day. The worst that can happen is that they won't respond. What is most likely to happen is that you'll become more confident, broaden your social circle, and transform your life forever.

Answer C is the hallmark of the Assertive Flirt. You speak

whether or not you are spoken to, and take it like a trooper when no one speaks back. You can communicate your feelings and read the nonverbal messages of others. Most of all, you know that flirting is a real skill that can make you more popular and more successful in the real world. I suggest that you use this book to add 101 more ways to flirt to your repertoire.

♥ **23** ♥

Heartfelt Tips for a Happy Valentine's Day

♥ Throw a casual "Meet Your Valentine" party. Invite every unattached man and woman you know (including those with whom you *think* you have nothing in common), then make it a requirement for admission that each guest bring along at least one available friend. Above all, make it clear that your party will be a singles-only event. Established couples tend to relate to people two at a time, and that can inhibit free and spontaneous mingling.

♥ Join a gym. Meeting a whole new group of people in the dregs of February can keep your heart healthy in more ways than one.

♥ Don't send anonymous valentines. Someone other than the sender invariably gets the credit.

♥ One woman I met recently told me about her most memorable Valentine's Day surprise. She was working as a hygienist in a dentist's office where a popular local radio station was piped in every day. One February 14th, she was delighted to hear that one of her patients had requested a song in her honor. The tune? "Make Me Smile" by Chicago!

Great Flirting Props for Mass Transit

"*I take a commuter* train with hundreds of eligible men every day but I never meet anybody!" It didn't take me long to discover why my friend Alexandra was having no luck getting her love life moving: As soon as she got onto the train she plugged her ears with Walkman headphones! Who would dare disturb a fellow commuter who had taken such pains to tune them out? I know I wouldn't.

Still, trains, planes, and buses can be great places to flirt. All you need to do is carry on a smile and a great flirting prop, for instance:

♥ A pet. I've seen many interesting people on trains, planes, and buses, but I've never seen anyone attract more interest than a young woman who boarded an Amtrak train with a gorgeous Persian cat in a carrier. Every cat lover who came down the aisle (and there are lots of them—cats are the second most popular pet in America!) stopped to admire the feline and chat with its owner.

♥ A schedule. Spontaneous "I-can-pack-in-five-minutes" types and busy business people on the fly never seem to have one. And it's a great way to find out whether that compelling someone in row K, seat 2 really is going your way.

♥ Something clumsy. For years a very well-traveled woman I know schlepped her suitcase on an ancient rolling carrier with a bent frame. Needless to say, it took a tremendous effort to fold the carrier at the airline gate and biceps of steel to unfold it at the baggage claim. I asked her why she didn't get rid of it. "Then what would I have to ask an interesting-looking fellow traveler to help me with?" she replied with a grin. She may not have been such a smart traveler, but she was certainly an ingenious flirt.

♥ 25 ♥
4 Flirting Props That Attract Men Like Crazy

♥ A book. No, I don't mean a romance novel with a bare-chested buccaneer on the cover. (Even if he had a billowy pirate shirt in his closet and some luck with a home hair-highlighting kit, could he possibly be as swashbuckling as Fabio?) Instead, try a book with great word of mouth, a controversial author, or an intriguing title.

♥ A unique car. A successful female flirt in her forties drives a 1971 black Mercedes Benz in mint condition. The car didn't cost much; she bought it secondhand for twenty-five hundred dollars. But it has paid her back many times over. The car has not only provided her with reliable transportation, it has also revved up her social life. Men invariably stop to ask what year the car is or if the paint is original. One savvy flirt even asked whether she changes the oil herself—a great way for him to find out whether there was already a "mechanic" in her life.

♥ Jackets and T-shirts with team logos. It's a wise flirt who wears her team spirit on her sleeve. Why? Because men love women who like sports. One look at you in your vintage Steelers' jacket and he'll know you're a woman worth giving up Monday night football for. He'll also know you'll never force him to.

♥ Food. I used to doubt that the way to a man's heart was through his stomach until I met Julie. Julie gave her business card to two eligible men and struck up meaty conversations with several more in the hour and a half she spent working the concession stand at her son's soccer game! When I repeated this story at a workshop I was giving, another woman chimed in to say that she had had similar success while passing out eggplant pizza samples at a local health-food store. The lesson? Stop his stomach from rumbling and he'll follow you anywhere.

♥ 26 ♥
4 Flirting Props That Attract Women Like Crazy

♥ A child. It really doesn't matter whether the child is your own or a borrowed tyke. (Isn't it great to be an uncle?) Just dress that four-foot perpetual-motion machine as charmingly as possible and head for the park or any other public place. Children are natural-born flirts. They always make friends when they play—and watching their antics makes interaction easy for nearby adults. A note, however: Many women—correctly or incorrectly—assume that a man who is sensitive to a child's needs is also sensitive to a woman's needs. If your motives are sincere, you'll do fine. But if you're a wolf in au pair's clothing, beware! You'll be dropped faster than a dirty diaper.

♥ Interesting neckwear, vests, or suspenders. These accessories offer even buttoned-up businessmen an opportunity to showcase their personal style. Best of all, because ties, vests, and suspenders are not worn directly against the skin, they offer interested women a safe focus for their admiring comments. One flirt I know has gotten great mileage from a Tasmanian Devil necktie. And Larry King, who is as well-known for his suspender collection as he is for his many marriages, certainly has no shortage of female companionship.

♥ A friendly pet. Pets are people magnets—and you don't even have to worry if your pet's nose gets cold! Just make sure that you engage your four-footed friend in a public activity that others feel free to join into. Most women will return a frisbee if it sails into their personal space (you can make sure it does!), but few will join you in a five-mile run with Rover—or enter into a rough-and-tumble game of touch football with a ninety-five-pound Lab.

♥ Cookware. Nothing arouses the urge to help in a woman like the sight of a confused-looking man with a compli-cated kitchen gadget in his hand. And how could it fail? Your very presence among the convection ovens and waf-fle irons implies that you are willing to take responsibility for your own care and feeding—and that's an attitude women are thrilled to encourage. So pick up the closest bread machine (food processor, pasta maker, or anything else that looks especially daunting) and give it a long, quizzical look. Chances are, a woman will elucidate. If not, ask an amiable fellow shopper if she knows how it's used. She'll appreciate your moxie—and the least you'll get out of the encounter is a fresh loaf of bread.

And what if she says she doesn't cook? Lay the appliance aside, wipe your brow with relief, and ask her if she'll join you at the nearest coffee shop. You're probably both hungry.

♥ **27** ♥
Spring Into a New Relationship

*I*n *Spring, the savvy* single's fancy turns to thoughts of . . . fresh ways to flirt! Here are some you may not have tried.

- ♥ Offer to organize your company's coed softball team. You will be privy to the home phone numbers of each player—and every scheduled practice or rained-out game will give you another reason to call! Just don't turn yourself into the George Steinbrenner of the sandlot. Flirting and softball are games. You'll win at both if you maintain a playful, noncompetitive spirit.
- ♥ Slow down and smell the flowers. Get out to the park or botanical garden. Promise yourself that you'll coax at least three conversations into bloom. Better still, plant a row of

unique and showy blossoms outside your home or apartment—as near to the sidewalk as possible. Flowers are wonderful flirting props. Get out and tend them. It'll give everyone in the neighborhood a chance to make your acquaintance. Or pick one for a lucky admirer. You'll make her day.

♥ Use April showers to bring May romances. One of the most charming and unforgettable flirting stories I ever heard was related to me by Ashley, a young personnel manager who could remember the employment dates of everyone on the payroll, but could never remember to bring her umbrella. One day after work, Ashley and a young man converged on a street corner just as the sky opened up. Not knowing what to do (there was neither a cab nor a storefront in sight), Ashley turned to the young man. "No umbrella!" she shouted over the downpour. "No problem," he answered, pulling a newspaper out of his briefcase. At first Ashley thought the man was simply going to offer her the paper to drape it over her head. Instead, he folded two sheets into a pair of neat paper hats, plopped one on his head and handed the other to Ashley. Did the hats keep them dry? No chance. Did Ashley and her friend look ridiculous? Absolutely. Did they care? Only about each other. Ashley and John were married a year later. And appropriately enough, it rained on their wedding day.

The moral? It never rains, it pours. Make the meteorological conditions work for you!

♥ 28 ♥
How One Smart Flirt
Slides into Baseball Season

*E*ric, *a Boston-based* flirt I met on an airplane, has had so much success with this strategy, he considers it his "season opener."

A week or two before opening day, Eric begins to patronize the hot-dog stand outside his office building. When he finds himself in line near a woman he finds attractive, he strikes up a conversation that goes something like this: "These hot dogs are okay, but they don't compare with Fenway Franks, do they?"

Whether the woman agrees or says she's never eaten a Fenway Frank is immaterial. Either way, Eric is ready with his answer.

"You've never eaten a Fenway Frank?" (alternately: "You're into bleacher food, too?") "Then you're in luck! My department has taken a block of seats at Fenway Park. I can get a few tickets for opening day. Why don't you invite a friend and come along? Here's my card. I work right upstairs. Call me if you're interested, okay? I guarantee you, it will beat eating on the streets."

Eric's season opener seems like a fast-ball pitch until you examine it closely. As it happens, Eric works for a large insurance company whose offices encompass the entire building. He knows that any young woman he meets right outside probably works for the same company. The professional connection, therefore ("My department has taken a block of seats . . .") is one she can trust. And because Eric has given his new friend the option of including a friend, she knows he won't throw her a curve once she gets to the park. To sum up: Eric's approach may not score points with the hot-dog vendor, but it's just the ticket for getting that first date.

One of the Best Conversation Starters of All Time

*M*y friend Richard went to the theater to soak up some culture. When the evening was over, he had also absorbed one of the best conversation openers of all time.

Richard was milling around during intermission when he noticed a woman across the room eyeing a forty-something gentleman at the wine bar. At first, it seemed the woman was just "window shopping"—studying the man at length but always maintaining a safe distance. But just when Richard was convinced she would never approach, the woman made her move. She walked straight to the stranger's side, smiled her most charming smile, and said, "I'll bet there's a story behind that ring you're wearing." Since there's a story behind just about everything, the two immediately became engrossed in conversation and never reclaimed their seats until the house lights went dark.

Should Richard have been flirting rather than eavesdropping? Maybe. But since that evening, he's successfully used the "I'll bet there's a story behind that ———" line to elicit conversations on a wide range of subjects, including a co-worker's book on out-of-body experiences (she had had a dream that seemed "uncomfortably real"), a young woman's vintage derby hat (she won it in a darts game in a bar in Boston), and a Shar Pei puppy (purchased by a woman who wanted to own a pet more wrinkled than she was!).

Try it—when you have plenty of time to talk.

♥ 30 ♥
4 Good Reasons Your Ex
Is a Bad Topic for Conversation

1. A lover who kisses and tells is less likely to get kissed.
2. Treat your conversational partner to a full play-by-play of those agonizing final four months before the breakup and she may decide that the real problem might have been yours.
3. An ex-partner who can't stop talking about a past liaison sounds like an ex-partner who isn't over a past liaison.
4. Remember that big, dysfunctional family your ex blamed for everything from her chronic nail-biting to her split ends? Your conversational partner might be one of them.

♥ 31 ♥
Embarrassing Moments in Flirting and How to Avoid Them

Learn to Laugh at Yourself

*I*t was 7:45 A.M. on a Saturday morning at the local U-Save and I knew she'd be there . . . she was always there, like clockwork, filling her cart with the staples of singledom: vegetables, yogurt, and orange juice (the fresh-squeezed kind you can only get in the produce department). I'd been checking her out for a month, and last week I'd had enough. I decided I'd speak to her. I checked out quickly, threw my groceries into the trunk of my car, and positioned myself in a spot near the door . . . the spot usually reserved for Boy Scout candy drives and Veteran's Day poppy sales.

It wasn't long before she came out, carrying a bag in each arm. While I groped for something to say, she took a look at me, smiled, and said, "I didn't get any change today.

*But I promise I'll give next week, okay?" I nodded like a
dweeb and all but crawled to my car in embarrassment.*

Lesson: I'm sorry to say you missed the deal of the day—the
chance to turn an awkward moment into an opportunity!
What do you think would have happened if you had laughed
at what truly was a funny, human moment, and shared the
joke with the woman you admired? Of course, she would
have been flattered to learn that you were hoping to collect
her phone number rather than her spare change. But she
would also have been impressed by your ability to laugh at
your own tongue-tied vulnerability—and that would have
made her more comfortable and relaxed in your presence.
Humor is a commodity that's in short supply. Use it to rise
above your own fallibility and you assure others that it's okay
to be fallible, too.

♥ **32** ♥
Are You a Self-Rejecting Flirt?

*You are at a night-*club. In the flickering light of the disco ball, you spot a nicely dressed man or woman standing at the edge of the dance floor. He or she seems to be alone and is moving subtly to the music. You:

1. Think about asking him or her to dance, but decide against it. People that fabulous looking are looking for equally fabulous partners.
2. Do nothing. It may not get you anywhere but it's less stressful than walking across a crowded room, asking a complete stranger to dance, and risk getting turned down in front of an audience.
3. Order another drink. This man/woman obviously knows how to move . . . and you're no Nureyev.

4. Don't give it another thought. Relationships that begin in a place like this never last.

The good news is, no matter which of these responses you chose, no one will ever disappoint, say "no" to, or reject you again. The bad news is, they can't. You've already rejected yourself!

Disappointments, turndowns, and even putdowns are a part of life. But they're no excuse for making negativity a *way* of life! The tips and techniques on the following pages will help you—and countless other "once-burned, twice-shy" flirts—to keep the fear of rejection in perspective . . . and out of your social life.

♥ 33 ♥
The 3 Most Destructive Myths About Rejection

1. *Rejection is personal*. Your train is delayed. Though it takes you forever to work up the courage, you invite that compelling commuter from car three to join you for a cup of tea. It takes her two seconds to say no. Was it your manner? Not if you were polite. Your personality? She doesn't *know* you. Your appearance? You look like a person who just escaped from work, not from a chain gang. So why *did* she turn you down? There might be a hundred reasons! She could be engrossed in her book. She could be anxious about missing the next train announcement. She could also be tired, married, apprehensive about strangers, sensitive to caffeine, or still reeling from the worst workday of her life. Whatever her reason, remember: She didn't really reject *you* at all. All she re-

jected was a cup of tea. And to take that personally, you'd have to be orange pekoe.

2. *People are rejected because there's something wrong with them.* Vital, attractive men and women are rejected every day, not because of their poor showing, but because of someone else's poor judgment! If he sidesteps you because you remind him of his twenty-three-year-old stepmother, that's *his* problem, not yours. And if she passes up an opportunity to converse, just excuse yourself and move on to more fertile flirting ground. Her reasons for passing you by may say more about *her* inadequacies than yours.

3. *Rejection is an injury.* Are you kidding? Rejection is a favor! Sure, turndowns sting—but they spare you the agony of spending another second in the dubious company of Mr. or Ms. Wrong. And that gives you the opportunity to get on with life—and the fun of flirting.

♥ 34 ♥
Strategies That Defeat Defensive-Dater Syndrome

Exercise #1: The Pity-Party Guest List

*I*nto each life, a little rejection will inevitably fall. But how can you begin to dig your way out of the emotional fallout of rejection when you're knee-deep in self-blame, feelings of inadequacy, and negative thinking? Try these:

Your best buddy throws a pass and, before you know it, he's scored. You just get intercepted. Other flirts seem to attract lovers at the drop of a hanky. All you get for your efforts is a dirty hanky. Right? Wrong! Rejection is an equal-opportunity annoyance. Everyone who's anyone has been rejected, some many times over. Like who? Why not make a list? Just be sure you have plenty of paper!

Magnum-hunk, Tom Selleck, was Bachelor Number Two twice on TV's *Dating Game*—and wasn't chosen either time.

Princess Diana, Loni Anderson, Lee Iacocca, and most of Elizabeth Taylor's husbands have gotten the heave-ho. So have Ivana Trump, Jeff Goldblum, Tom Arnold, composer Andre Previn, and "the world's sexiest man," John Kennedy, Jr. Wish you had a dollar for every time you've been turned down? Richard Lewis, Garry Shandling, Oprah Winfrey, and radio bad-boy Howard Stern have turned their rejections into very lucrative careers and are laughing all the way to the bank.

Why make a pity-party list? To remind yourself that, although rejection makes you feel like a party of one, you're actually in stellar company. And that rejected lovers can and do love again—provided they *try* again.

Strategies That Defeat Defensive-Dater Syndrome

Exercise #2: Imagine the Worst

M*y whole life is a* paean to positive thinking. I would still be an unhappy housewife today if I hadn't learned to transform my life by transforming my thinking. Still, as I explained to my friend, Evan, there are times when it helps to imagine the absolute worst.

Evan had been stymied by rejection anxiety for some time. At a recent workshop, he revealed that his fear of rejection had once again prevented him from flirting, this time with a woman he met briefly at his racquet-ball club.

"What did you think might have happened if you had asked this woman out?" I asked him.

"I don't know," Evan shrugged. "Something bad."

"No, I want you to be specific," I urged. "What is the absolute worst outcome you could possibly imagine?"

Evan considered the assignment, then broke into a broad grin. "She could have laughed in my face, pointed a finger at me, and announced loudly enough for everyone around to hear, 'Can you believe this jerk had the audacity to ask me out? Of all people! As if I would ever be seen in public with a wimp like him.' "

"That's a pretty embarrassing scenario," I commented. "So why are you smiling?"

"Because the woman I wimped out on flirting with is a very nice person, so, in reality, my scenario would never happen," Evan admitted.

"And if it did?" I prompted.

"I'd work on my swing . . . and on my flirting!" Evan grinned, "It's like what they say: What doesn't kill you makes you stronger. And although I thought it would, rejection didn't kill me."

Although positive thinking is the mainstay of the confident, emotionally grounded flirt, this exercise in controlled negative thinking can have a very positive effect. By allowing yourself to conjure up and confront "the worst that can happen," you learn two important lessons: first, that your fears may not be based in reality. (The object of Evan's flirtation wouldn't have dreamed of humiliating him in public; and most of the singles *you* meet wouldn't either.) And second, that rejection—even the most embarrassing, painful rejection you can imagine—isn't worth fearing at all. After all, you've already experienced the worst and lived to tell the tale. Real-life flirting can only be an improvement!

♥ 36 ♥
Strategies That Defeat Defensive-Dater Syndrome

Exercise #3: Develop a Risk-Free Vocabulary

*F*lirts—*especially* new ones—can get mired in the "risks" of flirting. But what do you really lay on the line when you approach a friend you haven't yet met? You don't risk your health or your life. The worst injury you can sustain is a blow to the ego, and nobody ever died from that. If you're a playful, prepared flirt, you don't even risk disappointment. Remember, flirting is the art of relating *without serious intent*. If you expect nothing from an encounter and get nothing, you've lost nothing. In fact, the most you can possibly lose by engaging a stranger in conversation is a few minutes of your time—and that's a risk you take every time you join a grocery checkout line!

The word "risk" conjures up thoughts of loss, insecurity, injury, uncertainty, and danger. Associating these dire consequences with the safe, happy process of flirting can keep you from doing what you want, accomplishing what you must, and getting all you can from your social life. If you are a hesitant or rejection-shy flirt, make a conscious effort to eliminate risk from your vocabulary. Instead of telling yourself "I'd love to speak to that attractive stranger, but it would be a risk for me," put a positive spin on your self-talk. Tell yourself that initiating a conversation would be "an interesting stretch," "a great opportunity," or "a welcome challenge."

Negative thoughts lead to negative action. By providing your inner voice with a positive alternative script, you will alter your perception of the situation. You will also minimize the biggest risk to your happiness: the risk of not flirting at all.

♥ 37 ♥
Tips That Cure the Summertime Blues

*T*anning is a health hazard. Charcoal is carcinogenic. But you can still add a little color to your life and cook up some fun by attracting and meeting stimulating new men and women everywhere you go! Here's how:

- ♥ Fly a kite! Kites play into everyone's flight fantasy, so go ahead and ask a likely copilot if he'd like to take the string. You never know what might take off.
- ♥ Go to the beach . . . but don't just lie there. Learn to body surf. Build a sand sculpture. Collect some shells. Just don't start a game of ultimate frisbee or football. All you'll accomplish is trampling sunbathers and kicking sand into their Slurpees—and grit between your teeth is not conducive to amour.

♥ Can't decide what to bring to the cookout? Opt for marshmallows. Toasting marshmallows is like administering a Rorschach test. You'll know before long whether he's crafty (two ends on his stick? He wants two marshmallows at a time!) or crusty (his marshmallow is burned black on the outside but delightfully gooey on the inside); whether she's meticulous (marshmallow toasted to a uniform golden-brown) or a charming klutz (losing three in the fire qualifies her). All in all, a sweet end to a great party.

♥ Opportunity may knock once but the ice-cream man rings at least fifteen times. Have money.

♥ The coolest flirting prop anyone ever used on me? A cheap, battery-operated, hand-held fan. It made me laugh —even in the subway in August.

♥ **38** ♥

Just a Simple Flirt with an Ice-Cream Churn and a Dream

*M*y friend Norm and I had just agreed that neither of us needed another thing, least of all somebody else's castoff junk, when he saw it at a tag sale: an antique ice-cream churn with a rusty handle. Less than a minute later, we were hauling it back to his cluttered apartment, wondering what he could possibly do with such an item.

What *does* he do with it? He uses it as a flirting prop. And very effectively. Ten minutes into any party, Norm has asked the ladies of his choice to begin cracking ice with hammers so he can pack it into the bucket. An hour into the process, he's met *all* the guests because each of them has had to take a turn at the crank.

Best of all, Norm's ice-cream churn was instrumental in bringing him together with a very special lady. You see, when the ice cream solidifies, it becomes difficult to move the dashers—unless a weight has been put on top of the machine to steady it. Norm asked a woman to sit on the mechanism while he cranked it. She agreed, the ice cream was phenomenal, and the rest was history.

What makes Norm's ice-cream churn such a peach of a prop? It encourages people to focus on something other than conversation, and to reveal themselves, as children do, through play. My hope now is that Norm will pass the ice-cream churn on to me. Then I can get *my* just desserts.

♥ **39** ♥

How to Start Your Own Fireworks on the Fourth of July

♥ If sparklers are legal in your state (even I don't recommend flirting in jail!) bring enough for everyone at the party to enjoy. They bring out the child in everyone. (And who could forget your name once you've spelled it in dazzling light in the air?)

♥ Even if you don't smoke, be the one at the party with the matches.

♥ If you're contributing a dish to the barbecue, bring something you can personally pass around. What better way to check out all of the "dishes" that are available to you?

♥ **40** ♥

Showing Great Form at the Gym

♥ Fitness-conscious singles invest a lot of time and effort into their workouts and they like others to acknowledge that their hard work is paying off. Compliments will get you everywhere!

♥ Your favorite body-builder may have a torso that looks like sculpted marble, but that doesn't mean he or she has feelings of steel. Don't be too personal with your comments. Instead of panting out, "Hey—nice glutes!" soften your approach by asking for advice. Say something like, "I'd like to get a little more definition in my thighs. What technique do you suggest?" Mr. or Ms. Olympia will discover that you are a discerning individual who can appreciate a toned body—and you will discover a trick or two that will add to your cache as a truly fit flirt.

♥ Be polite. Wait your turn. Don't monopolize the machines. And always wipe them down after you've used them. Gym members always know the Stairmaster hogs by name but not because they're popular.

♥ Most of all, don't get so caught up in your workout that you simply don't notice the folks who are trying to flirt with *you*. You'll never take to anyone if you immerse yourself in a book every time you take to the stationary bike. As for that Walkman . . . what would you rather hear, a reed-thin disco queen exhorting you to "work that body" or some real-life encouragement from a comrade in wrist weights? Think about it.

♥ 41 ♥

Embarrassing Moments in Flirting and How to Avoid Them: How Not to Use a Book as a Flirting Prop

"I had worked for an interior-design firm for several years when I decided I had learned enough to go into business for myself. I was trekking home from an appointment, my arms filled with oversized wallpaper-sample books, when I saw him.

"He was just the kind of man I always go for: tall enough to reach a crown molding without a ladder, the kind of beigey hair that goes with anything. I thought about saying hello, but he seemed preoccupied, like he wasn't in the mood for a conversation. So, rather than lose the opportunity, I did the only thing I could think of on short notice. I dropped the books right into his path, hoping he would help me pick them up.

"Well, I guess he really was preoccupied because he ended

up tripping over the books and ripping a hole in the knee of his pants. Oh, he helped me pick them up, all right, but the entire time he was muttering something about this being the perfect end to a perfectly rotten day. I never got a chance to give him a business card or anything."

Lesson: Many singles have told me that my first book, *How to Attract Anyone, Anytime, Anyplace*, gave them a sense of control over the flirting process. Unfortunately for you, heavy books—and a man's reaction time—simply cannot be controlled. Next time, just speak up and say hello. Love sometimes hurts but flirting should never be painful.

♥ 42 ♥
Sure-Fire Ways to Make Them Fall for You in the Fall

- ♥ Rake a huge pile of leaves. (To be really popular, rake his or her leaves!) Invite the object of your flirtation to take a leap.
- ♥ Warm up your new acquaintances. My friend Marissa, who has recently moved to New York from Florida, was tickled pink to be attending her first Macy's Thanksgiving Day Parade. Two hours into it, however, she was nearly blue from the bitter cold. Marissa was about to give up her spot on the curb for a spot of steaming tea when a man sitting nearby leaned toward her and said, "Excuse me, but you look very cold. Would you care for a 'hot seat?'" My friend was taken aback—until the man explained that a hot seat is a cushion that generates warmth. Before long, she'd accepted his offer, and an invitation to a casual lunch later that week. Although the relationship

didn't work out, Marissa learned from the experience: She went right out and bought herself a pair of hot seats, so she could attract anyone, anytime, and in any weather! The lesson? Carry an extra blanket. Or bring a thermos of hot chocolate and a few extra cups to that football game. Just don't leave your flirting skills—or that special someone—out in the cold!

♥ Follow the lead of the world's most natural flirts—kids!— and go back to school in September! But don't hit the books alone. Organize a study group to bring a select few classmates together. Or jump into a group project. It's a nonthreatening way to get to know that special student better.

♥ 43 ♥
4 Ways to Be a Fearless Flirt This Halloween

♥ The "Briefcase Drill Team" that appears each year in the Greenwich Village Halloween parade gave one flirt I know a ghoulishly great idea. She attended a party dressed as a high-powered executive (she even carried a bottle labeled "Prozac" in her briefcase!) and handed her card to every interesting man she met.

♥ Here's one for the Martha Stewart crowd: Pipe your telephone number onto candy bars with icing then wrap in plastic. Give this treat to the trick-or-treater you're sweetest on.

♥ For a costume others just can't keep their hands off, make one that's interactive. Frank, a man who attended one of my seminars, used an old refrigerator box to turn himself into (what else?) a refrigerator. Hungry women were opening and closing his doors all night! (Of course, he had treats to give them.) An added benefit: It's impossible to sit down when you're wearing six linear feet of corrugated cardboard. Frank had no choice but to keep mingling!

♥ Any costume you wear can be incredibly freeing to a fledgling flirt because it allows you to temporarily "become" another person. What woman wouldn't surrender (at least her number!) to a swashbuckling pirate or a Cupid with great pecs? What man could resist saving Marie Antoinette or being haunted by Elvira? Choose your costume with an eye to flirtation. (No priests or nuns, please. And no full masks. Prospects will want to know that you really *aren't* covered with warts, slime, or gore!). And stay in character.

♥ 44 ♥
Lines That Let Everyone Know You're in a Time Warp

1. "What's a nice girl/guy like you doing in a place like this?" (1950s)
2. "What's your sign?" (1960s)
3. "I can't explain it but there's something about a man in polyester that brings out the Gloria Gaynor in me." (1970s)
4. "Let's go somewhere a little more private and whisper some insider-trading tips in each other's ears." (1980s)
5. "Your condom or mine?" (1990s)

5 Despicable Lines No Self-Respecting Flirt Would Ever Use

1. "I love your earrings. In fact, I'd like to see them on my bedpost tonight."
2. "It's not often I see someone in here who obviously doesn't need to be carded. I hate these young crowds, don't you?"
3. "It's spring-cleaning time. Want to help me go through my drawers?"
4. "I love dancing with a man/woman with a little meat on their bones. It gives me something I can get a grip on."
5. "It's late. You'll do."

♥ 46 ♥
Exercise: The Sound Check

*G*ive a close friend a pocket tape recorder and ask him to tape your voice— without warning—during one of your conversations. Then tune into the tape for clues on how your voice or speech pattern might be affecting your flirting.

Do you drone on in a monotone? Researchers have found that one-note speakers are judged to be boring. Does your voice have a nasal quality? Although listeners consider these "heady" speakers to be nonthreatening, they are grating and could be a factor in listener turn-off. Do you speak loudly and rapidly—like, for example, a television pitchman? Then don't be surprised if your conversational partner suspects that you're out to sell her a bill of goods. And if you're a woman who's adopted a breathy, sexy tone? It may please some of the men some of the time, but most male listeners judge speakers with low-pitched, clear voices to be more mature, truthful, competent, and intelligent.

Embarrassing Moments in Flirting and How to Avoid Them: Personal Compliments

*F*or nearly two years *following my divorce, I avoided social situations altogether. Last week I gathered up my courage and attended a meeting of an organization for single parents. There was some socializing before the meeting began and I was introduced to Gina, a quiet, attractive woman who was a first-timer like me. Since this was a group for parents, I asked her how old her kids were. She told me she had one daughter who was nearly fifteen.*

"Fifteen!" I repeated, loudly enough to attract the attention of several members nearby. "You must have been a child bride!"

"Actually, I was a teenage mother," she answered softly.

After that, Gina retreated to a seat near the wall while the club members discussed child-care issues. I knew I em-

barrassed her and myself so I never went back. And I doubt Gina did, either.

Lesson: Religion and politics aren't the only topics that are too hot to handle in casual conversation. Ageism is real. And questions that compel a woman to reveal her age are never welcomed.

Although your comment was clearly meant as a compliment, it broke the age barrier. It also inadvertently called up another topic that is strictly hands off: Gina's sexual history.

As you already know, complimenting a complete stranger is an iffy proposition. It's better to keep the conversation going (and keep your foot out of your mouth) by asking a new friend some open-ended questions. In this case, you might even have focused on your own feelings and said something honest like "I haven't been out of the house since my divorce. You're looking at a couch potato without a couch." Gina would probably have been charmed. (Women love men who share their feelings!)

♥ **48** ♥
Flattery That Gets You Somewhere

Lesson One: Get Real

"Is that your hair or did someone scalp an angel?"

"My travel agent said I'd never experience anything bluer, deeper, and warmer than the Caribbean. Now that I've seen your eyes, I'm canceling my reservation."

"Call EMS. I'm about to die from happiness."

Insincere or exaggerated compliments are an iffy proposition. Many singles find such tributes embarrassing or even suspect. And because there is no way to respond to an obviously over-the-top compliment except to blubber out a "thank you," such flattery can actually inhibit conversation.

My advice? Be honest. If his eyes look more like mud puddles than limpid pools, he almost certainly knows it. And if her hands feel more like sandpaper than rose petals, don't tell her otherwise—she knows a flake when she sees one. In other words, if you can't find anything nice to say, don't say anything nice at all. Chances are you'll discover some unique quality you can genuinely appreciate about your new friend when you get to know him or her better. Which brings us to Lesson Two . . .

♥ 49 ♥
Flattery That Gets You Somewhere

Lesson Two: Personalize the Compliment

*W*e all want to be appreciated for the unique individuals we are. (Who wouldn't rather be the one in a million rather than one of the crowd?) So why not capitalize on this very human need for recognition by saying something nice you couldn't *possibly* say to all the girls/guys?

If, for example, he tells you he's a rollerblade fanatic, tell him "I should have known. You're such an agile dancer." If she volunteers for Habitat for Humanity, tell her how refreshing it is to meet a woman who isn't afraid to break—or to hammer—a nail. (Just think twice before blurting, "Oh yeah? I'll bet it's easy for you to find the studs!" Women are justifiably sensitive about sexually suggestive comments.)

♥ 50 ♥

Flattery That Gets You Somewhere

Lesson Three: Compliment the Things Money Can't *Buy*

In other words, don't compliment what a person is wearing. Save your kudos for the way he or she wears it.

Sure, he looks swell in his Cliff Huxtable-style sweater (wouldn't a mud fence look better draped in hand-knit, imported wool?), but those Aran cables don't really telegraph much about his taste. That cardigan might have been a gift from someone who simply couldn't bear to see him schlepping around in his favorite stained sweatshirt. (He might even hate it!) And watch those enthusiastic comments about her expensive watch or jewelry. She may think you're more interested in her significant earning potential than her potential as a significant other.

The fact is, anyone with access to an unexpired credit card (and not necessarily his own, either!) can buy a nifty piece of jewelry or a snazzy tie. You'll score more points by pointing out the way an accessory enhances his smile or brings out the unique color of her eyes.

Flattery That Gets You Somewhere

Lesson Four: Don't Hit Below the Belt

*O*r *anywhere near* it! No woman who has tried on bathing suits under fluorescent lights wants to know that you've taken an inventory of her breasts, hips, waist, thighs, or any other body parts that fall between her neck and knees. And no man really wants to hear that what you noticed first is the part of him that leaves a room last.

To stay on the safe side of the men and women you meet, keep your compliments above the neck. Remember: Everyone likes sex but no one likes being a sex object.

♥ 52 ♥
The Most Overused Line of 1996

"*Miss, could you* please lend me a quarter? It's an emergency."

"I guess so . . . but what's the emergency?"

"I promised my mother I'd call her the instant I fell in love."

♥ **53** ♥

What Promises to Be
the Drippiest Line of 1997

A *man at the bar* dips the tip of his finger into his drink, dabs it onto the sleeve of his conversational partner's blouse and says: "What do you say we take you home and get you out of those wet clothes?"

♥ **54** ♥
3 Reasons Why Dogs Are a Flirt's Best Friend

1. Dogs understand that flirts need to be walked. They will do what they must (and on your carpet, if need be!) to get you out of the house.
2. Dogs do zany, spontaneous things—sometimes to people's legs—that compel their owners into zany, spontaneous conversations they otherwise would not have enjoyed.
3. Dogs are inspiring, naturally adept flirts. Unlike lesser species, they are intuitive readers of nonverbal cues, they never monopolize a conversation, they don't take rejection personally, they can always tell a creep when they see one, and they aren't afraid to stick their noses in if it will help them make a connection.

A Short Guide to Politically Correct Flirting

"Beautiful people/ There'll always be someone with the same button on as you/ And they'll be beautiful people, too." The folksinger Melanie recorded this song nearly thirty years ago. And although the meaning of "beautiful" has narrowed in the last three decades, the message still rings true today. The people who share our beliefs and causes *are* attractive to us, first because we share some common ground, but foremost because the values we recognize in them mirror the values we appreciate about ourselves.

Being a socially aware flirt can benefit you—and the world! But only if you make like-minded prospects aware of *you* by:

1. Getting pinned. I know one flirt who goes absolutely no-where without a message button on her lapel. Political buttons are great flirting props because they reveal something about you and always provoke comment. Are you worried that your button will alienate a percentage of the electorate? Don't. The opposition is just as hungry for discussion as you are. Just keep the conversation light and you're sure to score points—politically and personally.

2. Taking your causes on the road. Sometimes I think bumper stickers and decals attract more attention than stoplights and yield signs! My retired friend Tommy agrees. He's been followed into rest stops by people who were attracted by the "Notch-Baby on Board" sign he's hung in his back window. Just don't take the "Honk if you're Anti-Fur" route. Your message may get a honk and a wave, but drive-by flirtation will get you nowhere fast.

♥ 56 ♥
Why It's Smart to Talk to *Every* Prospect at the Party Even If He/She Doesn't Appear to Be Your Type

♥ Because tossing a little charm into a roomful of people is like tossing a pebble into a lake: It has a distinct ripple effect. It really doesn't matter if you are focusing your flirtation skills on a single conversational partner. People who are open and friendly, who carry on animated, compelling conversations are noticed by everyone in the room. Spend a few minutes making whoever comes your way feel special and others will flock to find out what's so special about *you*.

♥ It's good practice. So what if that monosyllabic hand-model isn't date material? Don't wave him off. Practice your flirting skills on him or her and you'll be prepared for meeting someone who is.

♥ It's an opportunity to network. I know more than one flirt who shared a good laugh with an unlikely companion and ended up with a good job, a good stock tip, or a good friend. And friends often have other friends who might be more your romantic type.

♥ You might learn something interesting (what it's like to work as a roadie for Madonna) or useful (like where the hostess is hiding the really primo hors d'oeuvres).

♥ Because that unspecial someone may turn out to be the love of your life! How many devoted couples do *you* know who couldn't bear each other on first meeting?

♥ 57 ♥
Quick Fix: How to Mingle Without Staying Perpetually Single

I understand that I should speak to as many people as possible in a social situation rather than spend all my time conversing with any one prospect. But won't a conversational partner I found interesting think I'm disinterested once I move on to someone else?

You understand correctly. Even if the first person he or she encounters looks like perfection in an Armani gift wrap and orates like Frederick Douglas, the master flirt will *still* work the room. Why? Because the master flirt understands that you have to talk to a lot of frogs before you find someone worthy enough to share your lily pad. And because chatting for hours with a spectacular stranger only to find out that they're married, temporarily turned off to dating, or not your type is a waste of a perfectly good evening.

Still, just because you've moved on to another conversational partner doesn't mean you have to leave that intriguing acquaintance behind. You might say, "I promised the hostess I'd mingle, catch you later," or, "Interesting conversation, loved learning about your stamp collection, love to hear more," and then move on. Maintain eye contact with him/her as you meet and greet the other guests. Every now and then, look up from the conversation you are having and glance in his/her direction. When he/she returns your gaze, smile and look away. He/she will know that although you're temporarily elsewhere, your thoughts are still with him/her.

Of course, a thought without action is like a Porsche without wheels. It makes a good impression but it isn't going to get you anywhere. So before the evening ends, be sure to close the deal by using one of the tips you'll find on page 125. And if he/she isn't interested? Empty your pockets. You still have the names and numbers of the other guests you've met tonight, don't you?

Are You Getting a Fair Shake?

*T*here is nothing more
magical than that first physical connection between two mu-
tually attracted flirts! In nine out of ten cases, that first touch
is a handshake. Although we tend to think of a handshake
as a touch without intimacy, a person's grip can reveal a great
deal about his personality, his self-image, and his deepest
feelings about you.

Are you getting a fair shake from the men and women
you meet? These clues will let you know what people are
really handing you:

The firm, assured handshake conveys the message "I'm as
solid as a rock. You can trust me!" *Can* you trust her? Maybe.
This type of clasp is usually used as a business tool. Although
it inspires confidence, it also implies a certain professional

distance. Check for other nonverbal signals when you encounter this shake in a social setting.

The glad-hander's grip is the mainstay of the politician. Brief, firm, always accompanied by a broad smile and very limited eye contact, it is the mark of the man who plays to a crowd. Trade him in on a partner who's looking for a friend—not an audience.

The sweaty-palmed shake says, "I may look as cool as a cucumber but I'm a tomato under pressure!" Turn down the heat and make her comfortable. She's literally put her vulnerability into your hands.

The bone-crushing clasp announces, "I can't bowl you over with my electrifying personality so I'll overpower you with my grip." The crusher wants desperately to impress you. If you happen to be wearing rings, he'll undoubtedly make an impression.

The stiff-postured shake. Reaching for your hand without leaning toward you, communicates the following message: "I'll meet you, but I won't meet you halfway." Unless you're in the market for a partner whose stiff upper lip ends somewhere around his ankles, seek out more flexible flirts.

♥ 59 ♥
The Flirting Handshake

"*O*h, no . . . a handshake instead of a kiss!" Do you remember that line? It was the text of a popular breath-freshener commercial in the seventies. Apparently handshakes have changed a lot—and for the better—in the last two decades. As the flirts in my seminars have told me, a handshake can be a lot more stimulating, seductive, and sexy than a dry "Nice-to-have-met-you" peck on the cheek . . . *if* you know the secret to a sexy, stimulating shake.

What can you do to make interdigitation intriguingly *intimate?* Use the hand-over-hand clasp when greeting that special someone! Countless men have told me that when a woman offers her hand, then covers the grip with her other hand, it makes them feel important, enticed, and especially well liked. And the women in my seminars tell me that the hand-over-hand shake is their hands-down favorite, as well. Having them be on the receiving end of such a suave, almost Continental clasp let's them know they're more than just another acquaintance, and leaves them feeling secure, cared for, and "properly courted."

Or, hold the handshake a moment longer than necessary, and make eye contact.

Give these a try. It just might shake up your love life.

♥ **60** ♥
The Grossest Handshake That Ever Crossed My Palm

"*Oh, so you think* of yourself as a flirting expert," prodded a man I hadn't yet met at a neighborhood block party. "Well, I bet I could teach you something about flirting."

I smiled as pleasantly as possible. He might be able to teach me a thing or two about confrontation, but flirting? I had my doubts—still, I was intrigued. "Oh yeah? Like what?"

"Like my special handshake. Come on," he urged. "Put 'er there."

I put my hand in his expecting some form of a straightforward clasp. And for a second, he did grip my hand. But then, just as I was warming to his touch, he reached his middle finger between our hands and used it to stroke my palm.

I couldn't have pulled my hand away faster if he had plugged my fingers into an outlet. His "special" technique sent shivers up my spine, to be sure, but they were shivers of revulsion! In a matter of seconds, he had made me feel violated, sexually vulnerable, and unspeakably angry just by touching my hand.

If there are any more men out there using this slimy shake, please stop. It is neither seductive nor erotic. It's an aggressive, intimidating, juvenile, "terminator"-type technique—and nothing "terminates" a relationship faster.

♥ **61** ♥
Conversation Guidelines for Men

♂ Don't judge a book by its cover. She may have blue streaks in her hair and her conversation but that Cyndi Lauper image may be masking a rather conservative soul. (The same holds true if she's dressed in a staid navy-blue suit. Even closet grunge-band fans need day jobs, you know.)

♂ Remember that the authoritative tone that works in the office doesn't work in the social world. You might be able to tell your assistant to "Take a letter," but assume a bossy tone with a brand-new friend and she'll probably take a hike.

♂ Don't ask if she has children, at least not in the first five minutes. Single mothers are very sensitive about men who abandon the conversational ship the instant there's a blip on their "instant family" radar. Remember: This is a conversation, not a lifetime commitment.

♂ Laugh at yourself. When the male flirts who attend my seminars tell me how hard they work to say the perfect things and project the perfect image, I tell them about Dan—a man who charmed me completely just by being sloppy. I met Dan at a cocktail party where the hor d'oeuvres were served by white-gloved waiters. Dan carefully picked one up and promptly dropped it right into my drink! He looked up at me with a sheepish smile and said, "Did you say one lump or two?" Irresistible!

♥ **62** ♥
Conversation Guidelines for Women

♀ Spare him the details of your problems with your ex, your children, or your family. Your female friends may be riveted by your tales of "sturm und drang" but a male acquaintance will wonder "Aren't there enough complications in my life already? Do I really need to involve myself with *hers?*"

♀ Don't badger him about his personal thoughts. Ask him too many times what he's thinking about the party, the crowd, the food, the music, or the comment you just made and he'll soon be thinking that you're a pest.

♀ Don't play hard to get. Conversationally, that is. You may think that that bored, above-it-all look and those vague, disinterested answers are a clever way to mask your social insecurity but beware: There are too many fish in the swim for a man to waste time on a cold one. Men are just as uncomfortable in social situations as you are. Greet them with warmth, sincere interest, and enthusiasm and you won't leave every party wondering about the one that got away.

♀ Notice something nice about someone else . . . preferably another woman. Many men think that the difference between the males and females of the species is that the females have claws; that women are competitive, envious, critical, and catty. Show your conversational partner that you are confident enough to admire another woman's style or manner and he will see you as the gracious, accepting person you are.

63

Quick Fix: It's Critical Not to Be Critical

"*I'm a socially aware kind of guy—not in the flirting, you've-got-to-mingle-if-you're-single sense of the phrase, but in a politically conscious, get-involved way. An environmental group I belong to had just finished cleaning a local park and we were all bagging the last of the litter when I saw a young woman who seemed just my type: vintage John Lennon sunglasses, a beat-up denim jacket, the works. I went right over and thanked her for being part of the effort. Then, noticing the bag she'd slung over her shoulder, I said, "I wish you'd reconsider wearing leather, though. Animals should be valued for their lives not for their hides." She gave me a nasty look and said, "I'll bear that in mind . . . or does that cliché devalue bears, too?"*

Lesson: Anyone who's socially aware (and I mean in the flirtatious sense) needs to know that criticism is the ultimate conversation ender. Even if your conversational partner is smoking, ingesting enough blubber to feed an Eskimo village, or doing anything else you consider harmful, you can't expect her to welcome unsolicited opinions on her personal choices. Why should she? You don't really know the details of her personal life. Consequently, you're giving an opinion on something you know nothing about! Next time, keep your comments to yourself. You may save a whale of a conversation.

64

Quick Fix: The Case of the Vanishing Possibilities

"Last week I met a terrific woman at a party. I thought the two of us shared a special rapport. (She even joined me in poking fun at the pigs in a blanket! How intimate is that?) But when I scanned the crowd for her later on (the hostess was serving finger sandwiches!) I discovered that she had already gone. I know she enjoyed my company. And I know she appreciated my sense of humor. What happened?"

Lesson: Simple. Two people connected with each other, then with their fear of rejection. Each went away hoping the other would take the risk and reveal his interest and, sadly, neither ever did.

It isn't easy letting someone know you'd like to know him better—especially when you hardly know him at all. As a fledgling flirt, you are no doubt given pause by what you perceive to be a fifty-fifty chance of rejection. What you need to realize, however, is that the failure rate climbs to 100 percent the instant you let a promising prospect walk out the door without even knowing your area code!

Appealing singles are like tempting appetizers. If they look good to you, you've got to make your move before they disappear.

As for the odds, the clever conversation closers on page 125 can put them in your favor.

♥ 65 ♥
More Common Ways Fledgling Flirts Make Prospects Vanish

1. Stick your fork into his/her food. Among established couples, mutual feeding is a sign of intimacy and a sexual invitation. Among newly introduced conversational partners it is a sign of bad manners and a reason to abandon what was a perfectly acceptable plate of gravlax.

2. Be a hypochondriac. Reeling off a list of your vapors, chilblains, and suspicious symptoms has been proven to be detrimental to your well-being as a flirt. Quoting from your medical chart is known to cause lockjaw in a recent acquaintance. Don't be surprised if you find yourself in social quarantine.

3. Think of a conversation as a convenient opportunity to inventory your acquisitions. Your car, lakeside vacation home, state-of-the-art stereo system or collection of pricey Shaker furniture may be a measure of your suc-

cess, but material possessions don't ensure your success with the opposite sex. Charm, approachability, and a sincere desire to turn virtual strangers into fascinating friends is what separates the haves from the have-nots in the social world. So don't brag too loudly about that bigscreen TV with surround-sound. You may find yourself spending a lot of time in front of it—alone.

♥ **66** ♥

How to End a Conversation When You'd Prefer *Not* to End the Conversation

♥ "You are really a very funny man/woman. I know a comedy club where they open up the mike on Wednesdays. I'd love to check it out. Would you like to join me?"

♥ "You're a wonderful dancer. Have you ever tried ballroom/Western line dancing? I was thinking about taking a class and I could really use an experienced partner."

♥ "Your ideas on _____ were so fascinating I'd love to hear more. Would you mind if we exchanged cards?"

♥ "I really enjoyed our conversation. Let me give you my card and maybe we can get together next week. I'm free on Thursdays."

♥ "We work so close to each other. Would you like to meet for lunch one day next week? I promise, no pigs in a blanket!"

♥ **67** ♥

A New Year's Line That
Made Me Drop My Noisemaker

It was near midnight one New Year's Eve in the not-too-distant past. My date had gone off to refill our champagne glasses. I was watching the festivities from the edge of the dance floor when the count-down began.

I had just begun to look around for my escort when a very handsome man (with whom I'd shared a smile or two earlier) moved into the spot beside me and said, "I've heard that whatever you're doing during the first seconds of the New Year, you'll do throughout the coming year. If you don't mind, I'd like to stay close to you. You see, I'm an art lover. I want to spend the new year admiring classical beauty."

♥ **68** ♥

Quick Fix: The Hit-and-Run Flirt

"A few days ago, I opened my umbrella on a busy street corner and it instantly turned itself inside out. I immediately turned to a man nearby and said, 'My friends have always told me that I'm no Mary Poppins. I guess this is what they meant.' It was a great line. The man laughed. But when the light turned green, off we went. Why don't my one-liners ever seem to develop into conversations?"

Lesson: A thoughtful flirt never answers an anecdote with an anecdote, but in this case I'll make an exception.

It was a drizzly evening in Manhattan—the kind of evening when everyone on the street stops waiting for the bus and starts looking for a cab. Chilled to the bone, I decided to join the crowd. Since I try to make smiling a practice, I put on the most pleasant face possible and raised my arm. Immediately, three taxis pulled up—and picked up three people other than me. A damp but dashing man standing near the corner grinned at me and commented, "They stop for the cranky, blue-haired crowd but they won't stop for that smile? Go figure." Then he disappeared into the misty night, leaving me to wonder what might have happened if *he* had stopped long enough for me to pick up on his kind comment!

The lesson? Don't be a "hit-and-run" flirt. After you've engaged a partner in conversation, stop, smile, and give him or her a chance to respond. Better still, follow up your clever quips with open-ended questions that require something other than a yes-or-no answer. Remember: Speaking is only half of any conversation. The process is only complete when you've successfully encouraged your partner to speak back.

♥ 69 ♥
Outrageous Flirting Tactics That Really Worked!

The Identity Crisis

"*A few weeks ago I experienced a life-transforming case of mistaken identity. I was walking down the street when a woman I thought I knew from the gym emerged from a doorway ahead of me. Since calling to her several times elicited no response, I put on my best 'how-are-you-doing-old-friend smile,' ran up alongside her and said, 'What? I'm good enough to sweat with on the Stairmaster but now that you're in great shape you can't talk to me?' Of course, she wasn't the woman I thought she was and I apologized profusely but we went on to have a very pleasant conversation—so pleasant that when she sees me now she always laughs and says hello.*

Although that particular woman turned out to be married, the encounter was not a dead-end. I have since used the same ploy twice on women I wanted to meet. The first time was a strikeout. (Never detain a woman in an airport. If she has a prepaid ticket a conversation is out of the question.) But the second time I ended up buying coffee for my new 'old friend.' We discovered that we were both exercise nuts, that we knew people in common and, ultimately, that you can get as good a workout in a dance club as you can in any gym."

Lesson: Not even the best-equipped gym could whip an old and tired line like "Haven't we met somewhere before?" into shape . . . but putting the cliché into action really does give it a fresh twist! It also gives you an opportunity to break the ice with a complete stranger, charm her with a humorous remark, and discover whether she shares an interest in the activities you find enjoyable.

Of course, bounding up behind a person can be threatening, especially in a big city. Be sure to keep that smile on your face. It lets the object of your flirtation know that your intentions are honorable. And don't pursue the encounter if she balks. Forced conversation, however well intentioned, is never good form.

The Conga Line to Oblivion

*Why Weddings Are Difficult Places
to Flirt . . . and How to Flirt There Anyway*

*W*edding receptions are a problem because so many singles attend them in pairs. But are those couples committed? Some are. But many are simply hasty pairings between a panic-stricken friend of the bride and a conveniently underscheduled friend of the opposite sex.

Of course, you can't flirt overtly with someone else's escort. No amount of champagne served in a plastic glass is an excuse for bad manners. But you can turn a wedding reception into a flirt's buffet if you are willing to follow a few ground rules. First, if you are unattached, take the leap and go stag. (Whether you are attending the wedding of a family member or a friend, you *will* know people there.)

Second, take part in the festivities. When the Conga line forms (and it will), wedge yourself in behind a celebrant who compels you. (Avoid any who have accepted straw sombreros from the DJ. He or she won't remember you the next morning.) Line dances are one of the few opportunites where a single person gets to actually touch a stranger without breaking the personal space taboo. When the dance is over, make yourself approachable. Don't flee from the dance floor like Cinderella. Applaud. Strike up a conversation about absolutely anything with whomever happens to be nearby. Commiserate about the disappearance of the "Bunny Hop." Or ask if your conversational partner is a guest of the bride or the groom. If he or she happens to have been invited by the same "side," you can chat about people you might know in common. If not, let him or her know exactly how you came to be invited. Then, if your new friend decides to get in touch with you later, all it will take is a call to the bride or groom.

Above all, don't dive for the garter . . . especially if someone is still wearing it.

♥ 71 ♥

How to Make the Most of an Evening at the Movies

It isn't easy to flirt at the movies. For one thing, you really do have to keep quiet. For another, it's hard to make meaningful eye contact in the flickering afterglow of an on-screen train wreck. But here's an idea that's never failed to work for me.

Arrive with a friend and a tub of popcorn after most of the crowd has been seated and just before the feature begins. Seat yourself between your friend and an interesting single. Pass the popcorn between you and your friend several times . . . then, "inadvertently" pass it the wrong way. Whether your offer is accepted or not, he or she will be eating out of your hand before the credits roll.

♥ **72** ♥
Hot to Get Lucky at the Public Library

♥ Whisper to that friendly looking bookworm in the reading room, "I'm next on the waiting list for the novel you're reading. Is it living up to its reviews?"

♥ Use the copy machine as a flirting prop by copying something a bit out of the ordinary. A single woman I know who returned to college after her divorce developed a great rapport with a man in the university library when he discovered her busily xeroxing photographs of people's hands for a report on the credibility of palmistry.

♥ Or do your copying, gather up your papers, leave your finished copy in the tray and walk away. That thoughtful person behind you is sure to hunt you down and return it.

♥ Avoid any ploy in which you "mistake" an intriguing patron for the librarian. Librarians are a fascinating and passionate bunch but certain stereotypes die hard.

♥ 73 ♥

Weeding Out the Wedded

You're flirting. That certain someone is flirting back. But how can you be certain the object of your flirtation hasn't already met his or her match? Since wedding rings are as easily dispensed with as scruples, these guidelines will help separate the singles from the double-dealers.

♥ Get the scoop on his lifestyle. Does he own a minivan? If he's an electrician he might be schlepping tools, but if he's an accountant he may be schlepping a wife and family. Did he spend his last vacation at Disney World? (Hold on—he could still be a single father!) Ask him if he can recommend any four-star restaurants near the Magic Kingdom. If he can, he probably didn't eat there at the urging of his kids.

♥ Be alert to slips of the tongue. When describing where they've been and what they've done, marrieds can't help but use the word "we." If she tells you that "Colorado was lovely even though we didn't get a chance to try the high-altitude skiing," it's time for you to get into another lift line.

♥ Ask "Does your wife ski?" "Do your children go to private school?" Get right to the point.

♥ Know the "price of cheating." Does she know anything about car maintenance—or at least the name of a mechanic she trusts? If she's single, she should. Does he know how much common grocery-store items cost—or at least the name of the most reasonably priced take-out restaurant in the area? If he's responsible for his own care and feeding, he should.

♥ 74 ♥

Outrageous Flirting Tactics
That Really Worked!

The Free Ride

"*O*ne morning while driving to work on the Garden State Parkway (a highway known for its many tolls) my car and the Lexus in the next lane were both cut off by a speeding lane-changer. Not being one to suffer such indignities silently, I caught the eye of the Lexus driver—a dapper-looking gentleman—and threw my hands up in frustration. He smiled at me and patted his chest as though the close encounter had given him arrhythmia. Then he pointed to the dealer's sticker in the side window. No wonder he'd been so upset by the driver's recklessness. The Lexus was brand new.

We continued on down the road at about the same speed, exchanging smiles and glances from the safety of our cars until we pulled into line at the same tollbooth, his car behind mine. That's when I decided to make my move. I pulled into *the booth, handed the toll-taker a dollar, and asked him to deduct two tolls: one for my car and one for the car behind mine. At the next tollbooth, the Lexus edged in in front of me. Not only did the grinning toll-taker inform me that my passage was paid in full but he also handed me the man's business card. I called him a few days later. I expect to be in the passenger's seat of that Lexus someday soon."*

Lesson: Everyone has heard that familiarity breeds contempt, but shared contempt can also breed familiarity! In this case, an irresponsible driver actually did you a good turn by providing you and your new friend with a shared experience and an opportunity to make nonverbal conversation. Then you made the most of a potentially bad situation by maintaining the eye contact and making the first move. I say drive on, gutsy flirt—and full speed ahead!

♥ *75* ♥

Flirting in the Fast Lane

A *car is an extension* of an individual's personal space. That being the case, a savvy flirt would no more reach inside the open window of another person's Chevy than they would reach into the open collar of an intriguing stranger's shirt. But it is possible to make points with a fellow driver without adding points to your driving record. All you need to do is:

♥ *Carry a traffic-stopping flirting prop.* A woman I know who travels internationally every year brought back a fabulously funny flirting prop for her car from Great Britain: life-size cut-outs of Prince Charles and Lady Diana designed to be mounted in a car window. The cardboard couple's hands were attached to their bodies by springs so every time my friend hit the gas Chuck and Di gave the royal wave. The display attracted constant attention from passing motorists, people in parking lots, and even a state trooper. (Of course, staties have a sense of humor! Could they possibly wear those hats if they didn't?)

♥ Stuck in a traffic jam? Offer the use of your car phone to a frustrated but friendly looking driver nearby.

♥ *Get lost.* But don't just ask that handsome Exxon man or comely passerby for directions and drive off. Once you've found your destination, go back and thank him or her.

♥ *76* ♥
The Interoffice Flirt

The most efficient flirts know it: One of the best places to date, relate, and meet a mate is on the job. Where else would you find so many attractive, available go-getters who share the same field of interest?

It is a fact that countless happy couples met on the job or through their work. It is also a fact that sexual harassment exists. I am happy to say that the "fine line" between genuine mutual interest and humiliating sexual pursuit isn't really so fine to the five thousand flirts who have graduated from my seminars. They have learned that approaching the men and women they meet with manners, respect, sensitivity, and good taste is a tactic that works—in the office and out.

For those of you who have not attended my workshops, or who are boggled by the difference between acceptable and unacceptable office deportment, here is a brief rundown of the behaviors, gestures, and subjects that have no place in the workplace:

♥ *Personal compliments, no matter how innocuous they may seem.* When it comes to compliments, the office is a mind-over-matter situation: Unless you're complimenting the quality of a colleague's mind, it's not a matter for discussion. Limit your praise to his accomplishments, her efficiency, or other job-related issues.

♥ *Comments or questions about his or her personal life.* Her messy divorce, who he's sleeping with, and their extramarital affair are situated in dangerous territory. Don't go there.

♥ *Sexual subjects, innuendoes, and jokes.* They are taboo. Period.

♥ *Touching.* The pat on the back your colleague is looking for is never a physical one. Hands off!

Watch Out for Those Power Lines

*W*hen *it is free from* expectation or consequence, flirting is a truly democratic activity. Its goal is to effect a meeting of equals, both of whom share the same risks, rewards, and the same power to choose. But flirting can be a great deal more risky, less rewarding, and less democratic when it becomes entangled in departmental or office power lines.

Before you cross hierarchical lines to ask that attractive coworker out to lunch, *think: Is the employee someone who reports directly to you?* If so, he or she may feel as vulnerable to your personal whims as to your professional requests—and the resulting imbalance of power makes the relationship a no-go. *Are you comfortable with all of the possible outcomes of this relationship?* Look at him now and you see Mr. Right in a power tie. But what do you see up the road? If you can't bear the thought of risking your job for an interoffice liaison, or confronting a bitter ex every morning at the coffee wagon, then flirtation should have no place on your agenda. *Are your feelings one-sided?* Then give it up. Pursuing a coworker who doesn't want to be pursued isn't the hallmark of a persistent paramour, it's sexual harassment.

Power is an explosive issue even in the most balanced relationships. In the office milieu, it can blow you right off the corporate ladder. My suggestion? Lateral moves may not do much for your career, but they'll increase your longevity as a hardworking flirt.

♥ **78** ♥

Nonverbal Techniques for Professional Flirts

*B*ody language can speak louder than the interoffice public address system. You wouldn't be willing to announce your attraction for the entire staff to hear, would you? Then make sure you don't telegraph it with your posture, gestures, or movements, either.

In the office, your body language should be like your office door: half open so that others can approach you, and half closed to maintain your privacy. For that reason, I suggest that you:

♥ Keep eye contact light, playful, and most of all, respectful. If you've held a colleague's glance so long that you've made her look away, you've held her glance too long.

♥ Make sure your smile is friendly but not provocative. Sensuous smiles, preening gestures (like smoothing your hair or clothing), and lip-licking are simply too overt for the office.

♥ Trade in your usual hand-over-hand shake for a more businesslike grip. You might, however, clasp the hand of a special colleague a millisecond longer than usual.

♥ In an office setting, mixed messages are definitely preferable to overt. If there's a man or woman in your workplace who interests you, you can show your appreciation by leaning in slightly as you converse, then limit the flirt by turning your shoulders slightly away. Or you may keep an arm's-length distance while collaborating on that important project but extend an open palm when making a point. (A palms-up gesture signals that you're open for friendship.)

♥ *79* ♥

Flirting Props That Work

Your Disney memorabilia will look "Mickey Mouse" if your office is in a conservative bank. And the twenty-year-old Grateful Dead T-shirt you so prize might even terminate your career in sales. But subtle flirting props that reveal something personal about you without revealing too much of your private life *do* work in your favor at the office. Here are some to try:

♥ A photo of you engaged in an outdoor activity. A New York book editor displays a photo of herself taken while white-water rafting down a Colorado river. While the photo doesn't interfere with her professional persona, it humanizes her, gives office visitors a conversational "in," and helps to take the edge off of difficult business dealings.

♥ A pen you *must* have back. Businesspeople are notorious pen-lifters. Ask them to sign on the dotted line and poof! That Montblanc you won in the DAR essay contest is gone. Retrieve it with a smile and be sure to tell your office colleague why the pen means so much to you. Opening up opens the door to conversation.

♥ Things everybody needs. Not paperclips and staples. Everyone with a properly signed requisition form can accumulate his own stash of those. But how about a small candy dish full of mints (irresistible!), a needle and thread (unless you're a surgeon, *never* offer to do any sewing!), reference books nobody can function without, a computer program that makes short work of dull tasks, or a stress-reducing desk toy? (One flirt I know worked in an office where only management was allowed access to the coffeepot. He met nearly everyone on his hierarchical level by installing a small hot pot in his office.)

♥ 80 ♥

Exercise: *Playing Your Cards Right*

*B*usiness cards—whether they're the real thing or courtesy cards you've had printed yourself—aren't just for business anymore. In fact, smart flirts don't ever leave home without them. Why? Because calling cards last longer than a fleeting first impression; because they give the object of your flirtation the less threatening option of calling *you* (who doesn't think twice when a virtual stranger asks for their phone number?), and because handing someone your card is the perfect way to end a promising encounter without really ending it at all.

With that in mind, your assignment for this week is to give out as many of your personal introduction cards as possible, at parties, conferences, conventions, hobby shows . . . anywhere you share a conversation with a person you think you'd like to know better.

I have no doubt you'll be as successful as my seminar graduates who have parlayed the cards they've been dealt into many new friendships, great stock tips, advice on where to buy the absolute best bialys (that's what you get when you hand out cards in a New York coffee shop!), and, in one case, a job.

The One Card That Will
Do You More Harm Than Good

Certified sex instructor. Inquire within.

Go everywhere without it.

♥ 82 ♥

Don't Look Now:
Your Feelings Are Leaking

She's smiling as you speak. He's nodding at your every comment. This first meeting is really going well, isn't it? Actually, it isn't easy to tell. Although most flirts are basically honest, each of us have developed a vast repertoire of masking behaviors we use to hide our true feelings. It's a good thing, too. Few of us would be employed or named in our parents' wills if we always reacted with honest responses instead of appropriate ones!

But if everyone is as adept as we are at masking, how can we tell whether the people that interest us are also interested *in* us? By checking for what researchers call nonverbal "leakage"—the subtle physical signs that communicate a companion's true feelings despite his or her efforts to hide them. Signs like:

♥ The arm cross. She may be smiling but if her arms are folded defensively across her chest you'd better back off. You're coming on way too strong.

♥ The posture adjustment. If he stiffens or pulls himself up to full height, something you've said has literally "gotten his back up." If, on the other hand, he is noticeably slumping, he's bored.

♥ If he covers his mouth while he speaks or if she touches her nose after making a statement, your conversational partner might be playing fast and loose with the truth. Pay attention.

♥ Incongruous gesturing. If she's saying yes but simultaneously nodding no, she's either signaling an honest case of ambivalence or telling a lie. When in doubt, trust her body language. It is the most difficult to mask.

♥ 83 ♥
What Do I Say After I've Said Hello?
11 Foolproof Ways to Keep a Conversation Going

1. Ask open-ended questions. Avoid questions that can be answered with a simple yes or no.
2. Never respond to an anecdote with an anecdote. It reduces the conversation to a game of verbal one-upmanship.
3. Zero in on areas of common interest. You'll create an instantaneous bond.
4. Don't finish someone else's sentence. Interrupting is rude—and it cheats you out of an opportunity to discover what the speaker really thinks and feels.
5. Ask for other people's opinions . . . then don't argue when they offer them.
6. Describe your profession in a way that is interesting to others. Tell someone that you are a power-systems analyst and their eyes might glaze over; explaining

that you route the energy that runs their air conditioner will spark their curiosity.

7. If you are speaking with someone you have met before, refer back to your past conversation. You'll let your partner know that you valued his thoughts enough to remember them.

8. If your feelings about a topic can't be communicated in a few sentences, leave it out. A brief statement of opinion is interesting; anything more is lecturing.

9. Be willing to reveal yourself to others.

10. Make a real effort to remember your conversational partner's name. If you do forget it, remind her how memorable she really is by telling her, "Your story about _____ was so interesting to me. I just can't believe that I've forgotten your name!" Remember: A person's name is the sweetest word in the English language to them.

11. Don't be the sunshine of your own life. If you begin every sentence with the word "I" you'll have less chances of ever becoming a "we."

♥ 84 ♥

Fun Ways to Flirt at the Flirting Seminar

♥ Walk up to the prospect of your choice and hand him or her your registration form. When he or she registers confusion, say, "Aren't you the instructor? I'm sorry, but you look so charming and confident I just assumed you were teaching this class!"

♥ Volunteer for a role-play or an exercise demonstration. Role-play scripts are usually amusingly written. Consequently, even a tongue-tied flirt will come across as the life of the party who always has something clever to say. By volunteering to demonstrate an exercise, you'll showcase your vulnerability, sense of humor, and good sportsmanship. The entire class will feel that they've gotten to know you, and that will make you easier to approach during seminar breaks.

♥ Be aware of the men and women who might be flirting

with you! Fledgling flirts can become so caught up in developing the right smile, they don't notice the men and women who are smiling at them! A flirting seminar puts you elbow to elbow with scores of singles who *want* to relate to you. Tune in to their signals and this may be the last enrollment fee you need ever pay!

♥ 85 ♥

Don't Leave "Chance Encounters" to Chance

If you know she waits for the bus every morning at 8:33, if you know he hits the same newsstand every evening right after work, synchronize your schedules and put yourself in position to flirt!

One afternoon, my friend, Lynn, found herself in line at the half-price theater-ticket booth behind a very outgoing man. Now, the ticket booth sells discounted seats for every play on Broadway so the line is always very long. But Lynn and her friend found much to chat about. They discovered that they both preferred dramas to musicals. They even found that they worked in the same field (advertising). When, at last, the man moved up to buy his tickets, Lynn was in something of a quandary.

She knew she wanted to get to know her acquaintance better. But how? Hoping that their professional connection might bring them together some time in the future was too iffy. Asking a man she barely knew out for coffee seemed too forward. Many single people in Lynn's position would simply have let this promising prospect vanish into Times Square. But not Lynn. As soon as the man left the booth, she marched right up to the clerk and asked for tickets to the same play he would be attending. She also requested seats close to his. When the curtain rose that night, Lynn was in the row behind her new friend. And although he had come to the theater with a date, he and Lynn did exchange cards (for business purposes, of course).

Some of Lynn's friend's thought her move was manipulative; I think it was smart. Successful flirting—like any blockbuster production—requires preparation, forethought, and, sometimes, a little careful staging. Of course, it takes a little chutzpah to add this kind of drama to your life. But it beats waiting in the wings forever.

♥ 86 ♥
Flirting Doesn't End When Social Security Begins

*S*ome of the most compelling, honest, and irrepressible flirts I know have reached the age of majority more than three times over. What makes the mature flirt so special? They have the patience to charm rather than overpower. They were brought up at a time when couples jumped into conversation rather than the sack. They have a lifetime of experience to share. And, most of all, senior flirts have had lots and lots of practice! How do these seasoned romantics get out of the doldrums and into the social whirl? The seniors I know offer the following hints:

♥ Be a mall-walker. Mall-walking isn't just a workout, it's a phenomenon! What can indoor strolling do for you? Enable you to exercise your body as well as your social options, put you in touch with age-appropriate adults, provide you with a blissfully climate-controlled arena for conversation, and supply you with a nearly endless line-up of conveniently located eateries for quiet tête-à-têtes! Now that's what I call one-stop shopping!

♥ Don't discuss your aches and pains. Listing your minor ailments for anyone within earshot is depressing—for others and for you. Moreover, quoting from the Merck manual sends the message that you're not physically fit for romance.

♥ Don't make your dearly departed husband or wife a part of the conversation. One mention of the mate you've lost lets others know you're available. More than three mentions lets them know you're really not ready to move on.

♥ Get out of the house! Sure, you can bank, shop, and fill prescriptions by mail . . . but why isolate yourself now that you've acquired so much experience, wisdom, and freedom? Join the local senior-citizens center, enroll in a class, involve yourself in a civic organization, or just hit the streets. You finally have time to make friends with your neighbors . . . and good neighbors make for good flirting.

♥ 87 ♥

Are You One Foot Away from Commitment?

*O*urs is a face-to-face culture. Americans pride themselves on their ability to "look each other in the eye" and on their willingness to be taken "at face value." As a result, most U.S. flirts have become adept facial maskers, able to wipe their faces clean of nonverbal clues. How, then, can flirts from Maine to California accurately read the responses of others? By checking out those body parts a masker is least able to control: his feet!

Can you really tell the loafers from the well-heeled prospects by looking at his or her tootsies? You can bet your sole on it!

♥ If your conversational partner is standing with one foot pointed toward you and the other pointed out into the room, she is inviting somebody—anybody!—else to interrupt your conversation. Make tracks. She's not about to run into your open arms.

♥ If the person you're talking to is tapping or jiggling her foot, she's probably anxious to move on. Excuse yourself and give her a chance to mingle. She may be so impressed by your magnanimity that she'll find her way back to you later on.

♥ Small, aggressive foot kicks. Though his upper body language may be friendly, he's inwardly hostile. It's time to change either the subject or the partner.

♥ If your conversational partner is rubbing one leg against the other or smoothing his pants over his thighs, he or she is more sexually responsive to you than he or she is prepared to admit. Enjoy it! You've worked hard to become such a polished flirt!

♥ **88** ♥

Quick Fix: How to Ask Someone Out Without Really Asking

"I'm just too shy to walk up to an attractive person and ask them to join me for a cappuccino. Needless to say, I spend a great deal of time alone wondering what might have happened if I had! Is there any help for me?"

The fear of rejection, shyness, a lack of confidence, even a noisy environment can make it difficult to break the ice with someone we'd like to meet. That's why even I (a person who'd speak to a Styrofoam wig stand if I thought it'd talk back!) carry a Nicebreaker wherever I go. What's a Nicebreaker? A simple business-sized card that reads:

It's difficult to meet in a place like this, but I'd really like to meet you. Please call _____ .

A Nicebreaker, or any similar card that reflects your personality, is a great antidote to shyness. It eliminates the tongue-tied moment of confrontation so many shy people fear. (You just hand over a card and smile!) It also defuses the fear of face-to-face rejection. (Only you will know if the recipient chooses not to call.)

Best of all, the card-carrying flirts who have attended my seminars report that Nicebreakers really work. Some of the cards that have broken the ice for them are:

You are beautiful and I am shy. If you're interested, you can reach me at _____ .

and

I'd hate for you to disappear into the anonymous crowd. Please call me.

I suggest that you spend some of your alone-time composing one. To really score points, send one over to a prospect's table with a rose or a glass of wine. You'll soon be spending less time alone.

♥ **89** ♥
The International Flirt

"For Europeans, flirting comes naturally, but Americans don't know how to flirt," a German-born woman once complained to me. "They're simply too afraid of sex."

Any experienced flirt will attest that American flirts can be quite bold. Some could even benefit from developing a modicum of healthy sexual fear. Still, men and women brought up in other cultures do seem to be a great deal less encumbered by questions of protocol, fears about appearing foolish, or complimenting a complete stranger. They also seem to be schooled on charm and play their masculine/ feminine roles without the slightest hint of self-consciousness.

Europeans don't "practice" flirtation; they live and

breathe it! Here are a handful of tips to help you to breathe easier when flirting on foreign turf.

♥ Learn the language. At least enough of it to flirt! For a list of helpful phrases to add to your repertoire see page 177.

♥ Remember your continental manners. No, *Carius Granticus* was *not* the last known homo sapiens to help a lady on with her coat, pull out her chair, or hold the door for a stranger. These "old-world" niceties are still a charming fact of life in many countries. Make them work for you.

♥ Be a "Beautiful American." Shoving your way onto a crowded tube car may be accepted practice in Boston and yelling out your deli order may be de rigeur in New York, but in other countries these rude maneuvers are the mark of an "ugly American." A leisurely sojourn in an exotic locale gives you an opportunity to rethink—and amend —our everyday behavior. Make those positive changes while you are away and you'll be a better flirt by the time you come back.

♥ Don't be paralyzed by culture shock. I've heard it over and over again: A single American invests thousands of dollars on an exciting trip, risks life, limb, and baggage to transport himself to some fascinating destination, then ends up flirting with . . . an American he meets in the hotel lobby! Don't let a case of culture shock prevent you from making friends everywhere you go. Before you throw that AC adapter into your suitcase, read as many travel guides as you can possibly get your hands on. They will not only give you a sense of the lay of the land, they'll clue you in on the customs of the places you will visit. To further acclimatize yourself, read some current fiction or tune into the most popular films or videos of the country you will tour. Novels and films are a great source of insight on norms, cultural differences, and even current slang. You'll feel less like a stranger in a strange land. You'll also be less likely to embarrass yourself when you stop at that "lay-by" outside of London.

For specific tips on packing your flirting skills in that old kit bag, see the following pages.

Flirting in London

♥ Londoners are not buttinskis. They would no more invade your personal space, intrude upon your private thoughts, or interrupt a conversation in progress than they would smear chunky peanut butter on a scone. Nevertheless, they are extremely friendly and flirtatious once *you* have broken the ice. You may have to speak first but once you do, the conversation will outflow the Thames.

♥ The way a whisper travels around the dome of St. Paul's Cathedral makes this popular attraction an acoustical marvel—and a unique boon to flirtation! One smart flirt I know used the dome to her advantage by whispering the message, "If you can hear me, please wave." Almost immediately, two young men across the dome signaled that they had heard her. She beckoned them over, they exchanged hellos, and ended up taking the tube together to Madame Tussaud's.

♥ Go "local." In England, the "local" is the neighborhood pub—and it remains *the* place for casual socializing. Most British citizens genuinely like Americans (as one publican explained, "Americans and Antipodeans . . . they really know how to party!") so just go with the flow. I assure you, you and your fellow pub-crawlers will be exchanging stories, jokes, and personal data before you've finished off your first pint.

♥ Remember: Your accent is as interesting to Londoners as theirs is to you. Work this very effective flirting prop and you'll make your trip to merry old England a great deal merrier.

♥ 91 ♥
Flirting in Paris

♥ "Accidentally" drop something off the Eiffel Tower (only soft objects, please). This tip sounds a little over the top, I know, but it worked for my friend Denise and she hadn't even intended to use it! Denise was taking in the glorious view of the City of Light from the top of the tower when a gust of wind blew the hat right off her head. A gallant gentleman who saw the entire episode offered to help Denise look for it. They ended up taking an impromptu walking tour of some of the most charming streets Denise had ever seen. The hat, which was never found, was easy to replace. But to Denise the memories of that day are irreplaceable.

♥ Don't travel in herds. The French have earned a reputation as dauntless lovers but not even Napoleon would have been brave enough to invade a veritable battalion of seemingly inseparable women! Make an effort to see some of the sights on your own. If you're uncomfortable traveling solo, set aside at least an hour or two to sit by yourself at a sidewalk café. Separate from your old friends and give new friends a chance to approach you.

♥ Wine is one of the two things the French love best. So when you're confounded by the wine list, ask a friendly stranger for a recommendation. Then send over a glass to show your appreciation.

♥ Speak French . . . or at least try. The French really *aren't* touchy about visitors who speak the language badly, but they do take exception to English speakers who refuse to speak anything but English. Take a quick course before your trip. Or pick up what you can from Berlitz tapes. Knowing a bit of "the language of love" can only make flirting more interesting. And if you still find yourself torturing the native tongue, at least do so with a charming smile on your face. A smile is still the universal language, you know.

♥ 92 ♥
Flirting in Rome

♥ Eat! A proper dinner in Rome is a festive affair requiring many courses, at least two hours of your time, and several bottles of wine. Since the meal simply can't be rushed (dinner in a New York minute? *E impossibile!*) and because the good spirits just keep on flowing, you'll chat with nearly everyone in the trattoria . . . nearby diners, friendly waiters . . . maybe even the cook.

♥ Rent a motor scooter. They aren't expensive, they aren't hard to drive, and the best place for a passenger to hold on is around the driver's waist. What a deal!

♥ Hit the street markets. Italians are gregarious, touchy-feelie people who are intensely curious about visitors to their country—and in their colorful street markets they put these qualities on display. Stop to admire the eggplant. You won't get away from the stall without telling its owner the story of your life. Or take a risk and buy a bouquet of farm-grown flowers then present them to a particularly compelling stranger. Flirting is as natural to the Italians as breathing. He/she will be charmed.

♥ Italy remains an unabashedly paternalistic country. Consequently, many hotel managers and maîtres d' go out of their way to cater to single women who are traveling alone, providing them with high-visibility tables (better to see and be seen!), tips on local hot spots, and sometimes (if you're not careful) male companionship. Use this guideline at your own discretion.

♥ 93 ♥
Flirting in Hong Kong

The people of Hong Kong and Asia, in general, are thought by some Americans to be distant and aloof. In fact, nothing could be further from the truth. The men and women I met in Hong Kong are engaging, charming, and considerate flirts who relate to each other—and to visitors—in more subtle and refined ways than we. So how does an American who's flirting halfway around the world signal his desire to meet an Asian friend halfway?

♥ Don't wait for your new friend in Hong Kong to meet your gaze eye to eye the way stateside flirts do. Whether they're making a discreet, polite pass at you or merely passing you on the street, men and women in this beautiful country avert their gazes as a sign of respect.

♥ By all means, do as your hosts do and tone down your

own nonverbal signals. The singles you will meet in Hong Kong aren't accustomed to being skewered with an unbreakable stare. They simply will not know how to respond to such an overt expression of interest. And lighten up on your body language, as well. Don't invade a conversational partner's personal space, send titillating messages, or do anything touchy-feelie. If you're in culture shock and feel confused about how far to go, mirror your partner's gestures and behaviors. They are an accurate reflection of the current mores in this quietly seductive, urbane nation.

♥ **94** ♥
No-Fail Lines for the Flirtatious Traveler

People of all nationalities warm up to a visitor who speaks the language of flirtation. So the next time you fly the friendly skies, pack a few of these lines along—in the appropriate language. You may even cross the "international date line!"

- ♥ "May I help you with that?" (Consideration is a winner in any dialect!)
- ♥ "What is your cat/dog's name?"
- ♥ "If you were buying tickets to a play (or concert) tonight, which one would you recommend?" (Especially effective at a half-price tickets booth where a frugal traveler can generously reward an attractive "reviewer.")
- ♥ "I don't speak French/Italian/etc. very well but I'm doing my best to learn. Have I made many mistakes?"

♥ "I'm from _____ . Have you ever visited the United States?"

♥ "This country is famous for its _____ . Where do you recommend I shop for it?"

♥ "May I walk part of the way with you?"

♥ "I'd love to thank you for your kindness. Would you like a cup of coffee?"

♥ "Do you like to travel?" (A great conversation starter. People either love it or loathe it.)

♥ "You look too lovely to dine alone. Would you like to join me?"

♥ "Now that I've seen your smile, I feel *very* welcome here."

♥ 95 ♥
Guidelines That Make Breaking Up a Little Easier to Do

*T*he upside of flirting is that it enables us to meet and relate to more fascinating, eligible people than we've ever dreamed possible! The downside is that sometimes those people, through no fault of their own, don't live up to our dreams. How can a considerate, compassionate flirt unload a relationship that doesn't work without taking a load of flak, guilt, or anything else? Try these:

#1: Use "I" Messages

"You don't send me flowers/You don't sing me love songs . . ." Those and a litany of other liltingly bitter sentiments turned a Barbra Streisand/Neil Diamond duet into *the* anthem of the disgruntled lover. Although the song was a mammoth hit (what a soundtrack for a pity party!), it's a great example of what the sensitive flirt must *never* do when turning a soon-to-be-ex partner loose.

Beginning every sentence of your goodbye speech with a "you" message (such as, "You aren't my type" or "You always interrupt!") doesn't make for easy listening. For one thing, it places the blame for the failed relationship entirely on your partner's shoulders. It also delivers a direct blow to his or her ego.

Since you are the one who has diagnosed the incompatibility, it is only fitting that you accept responsibility for your feelings. Make a conscious effort to use "I" messages, for example, "I feel we have little in common" or "I'm not ready for commitment just now." Although this technique won't make the situation painless, it will leave your partner's ego intact so he or she can get over the blow and get on with life.

96

Guidelines That Make Breaking Up a Little Easier to Do

#2: Cushion the Blow by Saying Something Positive

*P*oint out something positive about your less-significant other before you drop the final bombshell. Just a word or two of acknowledgment (such as, "I love the way you make me feel so comfortable and cared for . . .") will make the impact of the rest of your message a bit more bearable (" . . . but I just don't feel that this relationship is working out for me.")

One warning, however: Don't try to fudge on saying something positive about someone else by saying something negative about yourself. Lines like "I just don't deserve a wonderful person like you" leave room for argument, and an impassioned discussion of your relative merits isn't going to get you out the door any sooner. What's more, self-deprecating parting shots like "I just don't deserve you" always sound insincere. You came into your less-significant other's life as a sincere flirt. It's best to go out the same way.

97

Guidelines That Make Breaking Up a Little Easier to Do

#3: To Spare You Both Pain, Don't Overexplain

*S*he'll ask. He'll nag. Your soon-to-be-ex partner might even cry, whine, or throw something to provoke you into revealing "the real reason" for your discontent. He or she is angling for a second chance. Don't take the bait.

I know it's tempting to tell her that her overwhelming need to control makes you feel like a marionette. But what are you going to say when she vows to change—no strings attached? And I know you're a breath away from telling him that you've had it with his chronic postnasal drip. But how are you going to cut him loose once he says he'd rather submit to surgery than lose you?

Her "silent treatment" or his tendency to read movie sub-titles aloud may, in fact, have driven you to distraction, but that's not what's driving you out the door. You want to end this liaison because it is not fulfilling your needs at this particular point in time. Say so, and leave it at that.

♥ **98** ♥

Guidelines That Make Breaking Up a Little Easier to Do

#4: *Make It a Clean Break*

*D*on't say you'll call if you know you won't. And don't suggest that you hope you "can still be friends" if what you really want to be is history. It can be very difficult to disengage from a person in pain—especially if that person has been a significant part of your life. But breaking off means separating yourself emotionally and physically from a relationship that is unfulfilling. Until you do, neither of you will be able to move on to more productive liaisons.

♥ 99 ♥

Guidelines That Make Breaking Up a Little Easier to Do

#5: Accept and Acknowledge Your Partner's Reaction— No Matter What It Is

*W*hile you must not accept responsibility for your partner's feelings, you must not deny their existence, either. If she is angry, acknowledge her emotions by telling her: "I'm sorry that you're angry. But it wouldn't be right for me to stay in a relationship I can't commit to." If he goes off on a "how-could-you-do-this-after-all-I've-done-for-you" tirade, sidestep the guilt. Just affirm his emotions by saying something like, "You're right. We've done a lot for each other. It's a shame we didn't connect."

You can't please everyone and still please yourself. If

your decision to break off a relationship leaves your partner with bad feelings about you, so be it. But if you make an effort to end the liaison with kindness and sensitivity, you'll have every reason to feel good about your honesty, your empathy, and your future.

♥ 100 ♥

Why You Must Never Give a Pest the Wrong Number

1. A polite, sincere brush-off might expose Mr./Ms. Not-Quite-Right to a few seconds of disappointment, but giving out the wrong number subjects him or her to hours —or even days—of frustration. If the chemistry isn't right, pull the plug on the experiment. A bad mix, under pressure, can blow up on you.

2. The idea that a refreshingly genuine flirt like you would deliberately give out the wrong number will be inconceivable to him. He will assume, therefore, that any mistake must have been his own and he will do everything in his power to correct it. If you are listed, he'll look you up. If he knows what you do for a living, he'll find you in a professional directory. If you met him at a party, he'll hunt you down through the hostess.

3. The creeps that go around, come around. If you bumped

into that self-centered, humorless woman at one event, you may very well bump into her at another. Only next time she'll be self-centered, humorless, and *angry*.

4. If you don't want to give out your own number, fine, but don't give out what could be someone else's! My coauthor, Barbara, recently found herself on the receiving end of at least twenty phone calls—all at odd hours—for a woman named "Bev." For the first week, the male caller insisted that Barbara *was* Bev. Then he began to accuse her angrily of "covering for Bev." It took the threat of legal action to stop the insomniac from calling. And to this day, Barbara interrogates every "Bev" she meets.

♥ 101 ♥
Make *Anyplace* Work for You!

It can be tempting for new flirts to save their skills for organized singles events where meeting eligible men and women is like "catching fish in a barrel." Is that a mistake? To find out for yourself, ask some happily committed couples to tell you where they met. The list you'll compile will read like a Yellow-Pages directory that's been fed through a shredder! The car wash, the veterinary clinic, the shoemaker's, the acupuncturist's, the library, at a salad bar, in the gym Jacuzzi, at the motorcycle races . . . these aren't just places where busy singles make a ten-minute stop—they're the places where smart flirts make connections that last a lifetime! And that's just the beginning. The more than five thousand men and women who have graduated from my seminars have met their match in locations that range from the ridiculous (clown college, Halloween parades, and talk-show tapings) to the sublime (the observation deck of the Sears Tower). And you can do it, too, if you are creative, open-minded, and bold enough to make wherever you are work for you.

How do you turn an everyday locale into an adventure in flirting? These guidelines will get your trip off to a good start:

Be aware of where you are. If you trudge the same route day after day, never noticing anything that's going on around you, it's time to open your eyes! That window washer thirty stories up, the grate that bit off the heel of your shoe, a beautifully decorated storefront, or even the construction site that's forced you off the sidewalk every day for the last three months can be a conversation starter, provided that you notice them and . . .

Share your thoughts with whoever is lucky enough to be nearby.

One afternoon I boarded what I thought was a crosstown bus and happened onto the most gorgeous man I had seen in months. He had the rugged good looks of Clint Eastwood, eyes that were Paul-Newman blue . . . and I, for once, couldn't think of a single clever thing to say! I headed past him toward my usual seat—the very last one, the seat directly above the back wheel—and like the seasoned New Yorker I am, felt it with my hand. "It's my favorite seat," I commented aloud to no one in particular, "but today it's too hot."

"It's my favorite seat, too," the man answered, to my surprise and delight.

From that point on, we were off and running. I asked him how his long legs could possibly fit into that tiny space. He answered that that particular seat allowed him to stretch his legs into the aisle without disturbing anyone. I noted that he had a slight accent. He told me that he was from Nashville. The next thing we knew, we were so deep in conversation that neither of us noticed that we weren't on a crosstown bus at all—and that we were both many stops past our destinations. Before we went our separate ways, I gave him my card. Although nothing came of the encounter, I will always remember it—and the important lesson it taught me.

The lesson? Go public with those clever (and even not so clever) one-liners and astute observations that flash into your mind! If your thoughts are amusing to you, there's every possibility they'll rouse a chuckle out of someone else, too. And if they don't? Just smile and go on your way. There's always a more receptive audience right around the corner for a witty, confident flirt.

Ask Questions. People who do the most flirting know that it pays to ask questions—particularly those that can't be answered with a simple yes or no. So the next time you're stuck in the inspection line at the DMV, don't turn up the radio. Ask that sporty model in the next car if it always takes this long to get rejected. (Your car might but you won't!) And wherever you might be, *always* ask about that unusual ring she's wearing or the book he's carrying. It just might be a flirting prop!

Most of all, *enjoy yourself*—whatever you happen to be doing, wherever you happen to be. Enthusiasm is contagious—and you have a great deal to be enthusiastic about. In the time it's taken you to read this book, you've learned to decipher the body language of others and send powerful nonverbal signals of your own; you've added to your supply of fascinating, creative companions—and learned how to say goodbye to those who are not. Most of all, you've mastered 101 new ways to attract anyone you choose, anyplace you happen to be. That means that wherever you are, you're in fertile flirting territory. Enjoy.

- ♥ Pay attention to flirting.
- ♥ Feel that it's okay—even important to flirt.
- ♥ Have at least five social interests to call upon.
- ♥ Remember that flirting is an action verb. Just do it!

Author's Note

Susan Rabin hopes you laughed, learned, and enjoyed *101 Ways to Flirt*. Happy flirting!

Susan Rabin is president of **Dynamic Communications,** a company dedicated to Building Better Relationships. Susan is a Relationship Counselor, a Cognitive Therapist and a Business Coach in Personal Effectiveness and Interpersonal Skills.

In addition, Susan is the founder of the New York–based "School of Flirting,®" www.schoolofflirting.com

Susan offers books and tapes, and is available for lectures, seminars, counseling and coaching.

Susan would love to hear some of your successful flirting stories. Anyone with a great story should send a letter in an envelope marked "Flirting Stories" to the address on the facing page.

Her other books, *How to Attract Anyone, Anytime, Anyplace* and *Cyberflirt*, are available at book stores and from Penguin Putnam at (800) 253-6476.

Example of Nicebreaker Meeting Card

It's difficult to meet in a place like this, but I'd really like to meet you.
Please call:

_____

𝒩ICEBREAKERS™
SUSAN G. RABIN, M.A. P.O. BOX 660 N.Y., NY 10028 © 1990